WRITING FRAMES
made easy

**Creative support
for primary writing**

Steve Mynard and Sandy Stockwell

pfp
teacherbooks

Creative support for primary writing

Writing is the poor relation when it comes to the development of literacy skills. Reading development has always been one step ahead but now there is a gulf and this has become transparently clear to us all with the publication of end of key stage test results.

A careful and considered use of writing frames throughout the primary years will help to address this.

This resource aims to support teachers practising in both Key Stage 1 and Key Stage 2 classes. It addresses the requirements of the English National Curriculum and the National Literacy Strategy Framework for teaching as it explores the range of writing to be taught, both fiction and non-fiction. This range includes argument and discussion, explanation, instruction, narrative, poetry, recount and report. A full explanation of each of these writing genres is given and 84 photocopiable writing frames are provided to support children in becoming independent and confident writers.

Writing Frames Made Easy also provides the essential background information you need to support the creative use of writing frames in the classroom and equips both teachers and children with the skills to generate their own writing frames.

In addition, this resource supports cross-curricular work by identifying links with the QCA schemes of work for design and technology, geography, history, information technology and science.

Both the publishers and authors hope that you find *Writing Frames Made Easy* useful and welcome your comments or suggestions for improvement or extension of the resource.

© pfp publishing ltd 2001, 2003
Written by Steve Mynard and Sandy Stockwell
Illustrations by Bob Farley of GCI and Sam Banfield
Cover design by PinkFrog

First published 2001
Second edition 2003

pfp publishing ltd
61 Gray's Inn Road
London WC1X 8TH

pfp orders and customer service
Freepost Lon20579
London WC1X 8BR
Tel: 0845 602 4337
Fax: 0845 602 4338

www.pfp-publishing.com

Printed in the UK

ISBN 1 874050 79 1

A catalogue record for this book is available from the British Library

pfp

Contents

pfp © pfp 2001 ISBN 1 874050 79 1 pfp, 61 Gray's Inn Road, London WC1X 8TH May be photocopied for use within the purchasing institution only.

WRITING FRAMES MADE EASY • Contents • page 2 of 2

© pfp 2001 ISBN 1 874050 79 1 pfp, 61 Gray's Inn Road, London WC1X 8TH May be photocopied for use within the purchasing institution only.

Teaching guidance

How to use this resource

This file provides a complete resource for teachers who want to use writing frames to maximum effect in the classroom.

Teaching guidance section

The teaching guidance pages provide a clear rationale for using writing frames – why, how and when they should be used. Ways of meeting the needs of all children are explored and the role of the teacher is identified. Models are provided for using writing frames within the literacy hour and for helping children generate their own. The emphasis is on using writing frames flexibly. These pages also provide suggestions for using ICT and for making cross-curricular links.

They are followed by an explanation of each writing genre referred to in this resource and an accompanying case study. The genres are *recount*, *report*, *explanation*, *instruction*, *persuasion and discussion*, *poetry* and *narrative*.

Key Stages 1 and 2 sections

The key stage links tables at the beginning of these sections clearly identify connections between the specified writing genre, the National Literacy Strategy Framework and the QCA schemes of work. This means you can quickly identify appropriate writing frames whether your starting point is a literacy objective or another curriculum area. You can also see the range of writing frames available to support each writing genre so you can locate further examples to reinforce classwork or to provide differentiation.

The Key Stage 1 and Key Stage 2 resource pages provide photocopiable writing frames in sets of three. There are either three different frames to support one writing genre or three differentiated versions of one frame. Each set is introduced by a page of teachers' notes.

Every teachers' notes page

- identifies the relevant National Literacy Strategy reading and writing objectives
- identifies links with the QCA schemes of work
- provides differentiated teaching activities
- suggests teaching points
- demonstrates how to use the writing frames within the context of the literacy hour
- suggests activities with links to areas such as ICT, homework and links to INSET.

What is a writing frame?

A writing frame is a simple model of how to write a particular type of text. It is likely to provide sentence starters, usually at the beginning of a new paragraph, to structure the writing. Children complete the sentences and then go on to write the rest of the paragraph. Writing frames also provide vocabulary that matches the text type. The long term aim is to develop children's ability to write independently in a range of styles.

Photocopiable writing frames resources such as this are readily available but writing frames can also be generated by children and teachers working together.

Why should I use writing frames?

Writing frames support children's early, tentative attempts to write in a new style. Like other types of 'scaffolding', they are removed once the child no longer needs them.

When learning a new skill we all benefit from being shown how, before being expected to do it alone. Learning theories remind us that children learn best when they work with 'expert' adults who can support their learning as they move to a new skill. Writing frames support this by providing scaffolding. They can be jointly constructed by the teacher and children and they act as a support by being a model of 'how to do it'.

The purposes of writing frames

Writing frames have a range of different purposes. They help children to

- extend their reading and writing
- focus on a specific writing genre
- reflect on a range of writing genres
- analyse writing for different purposes
- evaluate writing
- reorder what they have read in a text
- represent information in a new format
- be motivated
- experience early success in writing
- sustain writing.

Writing frames help children to achieve these things by

- providing a supportive structure
- providing prompts such as sentence beginnings or connectives.

When exploring a new text type, writing frames can be used to focus on

- the purpose of the text
- the intended audience
- writing structure and organisation
- text layout
- the register of the text
- the tense of the text
- the use of grammar
- the use of punctuation
- word order
- the use of subject specific vocabulary
- the use of word classes such as connectives

– or any other specific characteristic of the text.

The photocopiable writing frames provided with this resource enable you to support children in these ways.

When to use a writing frame

As with any resource, for the greatest impact use writing frames with discrimination.

Give them to a child, group or whole class

- when attempting a new writing genre for the first time
- when the children demonstrate a lack of understanding of a specific writing form, for example starting their writing as a science report and ending it as a narrative
- as a reminder of previous learning when revisiting a writing form.

Use them with a child who

- is overly reliant on writing in one particular style, perhaps narrative
- overuses some phrases such as 'and then'
- is reluctant to write when faced with a blank piece of paper.

Avoid using them once children are familiar with the text type and have gained the skills and knowledge to write independently in the given writing form.

Meeting the needs of all children

Writing frames provide effective learning opportunities for all children – they widen the writing experiences of children at all levels. They can be designed to offer challenge as well as support and can be differentiated by content or structure.

Using the frames flexibly

Use the frames as

- an ideas bank for teachers
- a model of the features of specific texts
- a resource for individuals and groups

WRITING FRAMES MADE EASY • **Teaching guidance** • page 2 of 6

© pfp 2001 ISBN 1 874050 79 1   pfp, 61 Gray's Inn Road, London WC1X 8TH May be photocopied for use within the purchasing institution only. pfp

- a draft version – start with the published frames then change them to meet the needs of your children
- a support for children drafting their own
- display – enlarged onto A3 paper.

Remember that the published writing frame is only the starting point in the learning process. Rather than a photocopiable worksheet it is a teaching tool that will help children become independent writers and take responsibility for their own learning. More detailed suggestions for using the frames in this way is provided on the teachers' notes that accompany each set of writing frames provided with this resource.

Working with children to produce their own writing frames

Children learn to become writers by first becoming readers. To support children writing in different styles and forms, share with them good quality texts that model different features. Direct their attention to these and support their efforts to write. Now the children can learn about writing by writing themselves.

The following is a model for producing a writing frame and subsequently encouraging independent writing.

Step 1 Read and discuss

Read and discuss a number of good examples of the text type. Encourage children's responses to the text and guide a discussion to identify the intended audience and the purpose of the text.

Finally, evaluate how effective the text is in meeting the needs of the audience and how well it fulfils its purpose.

Step 2 Deconstruct a text

Select one text to 'deconstruct'. Use this as a model. Read this text together and then ask questions to identify its common features.

These features are likely to include

- purpose and audience
- text structure, organisation and layout
- register and tense
- grammar, punctuation and word order
- subject specific vocabulary
- word classes such as connectives.

For example, a recipe informs a cook – it contains sequential instructions and is written in the present tense. It includes imperative verbs such as 'stir' and 'mix' and it might contain time connectives such as 'first' and 'then'.

Use a range of interactive activities to investigate the text.

- Place an acetate sheet over the text and mark specific features – identify and label them. Use the acetate as a visual outline that can be used as a model for the children's writing.
- Photocopy the text, cut it up and distribute its main parts. The children can identify each part of the text as a specific feature, such as 'title', 'heading', 'introductory statement' and 'closing statement' and put them in the correct order.
- Provide the children with a copy of the text and labels for the specific features. Children can match the labels to the text.
- Cover features of the text and ask children to predict what they are before revealing them.
- Provide children with a list of the key features of the chosen text and a photocopy of the text. They can then use highlighter pens to mark the specific features.

Step 3 Create a checklist

The features that have been identified by any of these methods can then be listed to produce a 'features checklist' for the specific writing form. The checklist can be compared against other examples of the same text type to confirm which features are essential in this type of writing.

Step 4 Create the writing frame

The final features checklist can be subsequently written up as a writing frame.

Step 5 Model the writing

Using the writing frame as a guide, the teacher can then model how to complete it. The teacher could offer suggestions and model the writing. The children can also suggest what to write.

Avoid asking children to use the writing frame independently or to construct their own frame until they can confidently use it during shared or guided sessions.

Step 6 Use the frame

The children can then use the writing frame themselves and produce independent pieces of writing in the new genre.

Step 7 Write independently

Once familiar with the features of the text, the children can then attempt writing in the genre without the support of the frame.

Working with writing frames in the literacy hour

During shared reading

- explore the shared text and identify its specific features.

During shared writing

- jointly construct the writing frame
- compare the features against the frame
- model the completion of the writing frame
- reconstruct the text, using the writing frame.

During word and sentence level work

- explore specific language features of the text.

During guided reading support children in

- identifying the specific features of the texts
- reading a range of text types
- evaluating the effectiveness of texts.

During guided writing support children in

- constructing their own writing frame
- comparing the list of features against their own writing frame
- completing the writing frame.

Once children are confident, encourage them to write without the writing frame.

During independent work children can

- complete the writing frame in pairs, groups or individually
- generate their own writing frames.

Once they are confident with the writing format, children can write in the given style, without the support of the writing frame.

During the plenary

- evaluate the published writing frames and self-generated writing frames
- reflect on the effectiveness of the finished writing
    - does it contain the necessary text features?
    - does it meet its purpose and is it easy to read?
- encourage children to identify their own learning and progress.

The teachers' notes that accompany the writing frames provide further suggestions for different elements of the literacy hour.

Assessment

You can assess

- independent writing to identify what writing frames they need to use
- completion of writing frames and their subsequent independent writing to identify when they no longer need writing frames
- understanding of writing by listening to them talking about writing
- application of writing skills outside the literacy hour in other curriculum areas.

Writing frames and the use of ICT

Computers can support the generation and completion of writing frames. In addition, children can read a range of texts on the computer and identify their key features. Computers can be used during shared and independent sessions for the following activities.

- Drafting, editing and refining both writing frames and children's own independent writing.
- Completing writing frames.
- Publishing completed work.

© pfp 2001 ISBN 1 874050 79 1   pfp, 61 Gray's Inn Road, London WC1X 8TH May be photocopied for use within the purchasing institution only.

The role of the teacher

Help children get the most from working with writing frames – use them flexibly and creatively and only when needed.

Provide purpose and audience

To follow are some examples that help provide purpose and audience for the children.

- Use the frames to write an explanation following an experiment in science or write a recount following a school trip.

- Write for a real audience such as a school visitor or children in another class.

- Regularly 'publish' children's writing by putting it on display for others to read.

- Make the focus and purpose of the activity clear. Check that your class understands what they are learning and why.

Explicitly teach the features of texts

Use the writing frames to teach children the features of different text types as contained in genre explanation pages and case studies (see pp11–24).

Model the writing process

Model how to

- spot features in the shared text
- construct and complete a writing frame
- write without a writing frame
- draft, edit, revise and publish writing.

Model the writing on the board, flipchart or straight onto an OHT. This enables children to see the writing emerging on the screen and you can demonstrate editing as you go.

Provide good quality texts to demonstrate what you want children to learn.

Encourage collaboration and interaction

You can encourage collaboration and interaction in the following ways.

- Generate a writing frame – set up the activity as a problem-solving activity.

- Encourage children to share their ideas and opinions with you and with their peers. Provide opportunities for discussion.

Draw on previous experience

Identify what children know about writing or about the particular text type. Compare this knowledge with their new knowledge, for example how does a report differ from an explanation? Have they read a text that was trying to persuade them to buy something?

Provide time

Throughout the literacy hour, provide time for practising, refining and reflecting.

Use opportunities across the curriculum to enable children to write in different forms.

Writing frames can enable children to focus on specific aspects of the writing such as content, coherence, layout, audience, organisation and language features. It may be that other skills such as handwriting, spelling or presentation may 'dip' while they concentrate on the new skill.

Cross-curricular links

Children are often more confident in one type of writing than another and tend to fall back onto what is safe. With opportunities to explore different text types they can experiment with and develop new styles. Extending literacy into other areas provides opportunities for this.

During the literacy hour children acquire essential and transferable skills that enable them to access all areas of the curriculum.

Links during the literacy hour

Scan the National Literacy Strategy Framework and find opportunities for cross-

curricular texts to be used within the literacy hour. Identify relevant links with the school's present cycle of topics. For example, using non-fiction texts related to the Romans when studying the Romans in history. Use cross-curricular texts for shared, guided and independent work.

Remember that during literacy time the focus must be on the text type as opposed to the content. Children will be looking at style, layout and use of vocabulary. Focus on the literacy skill rather than on the content.

The following are some ideas for using cross-curricular writing frames.

- When you know that children are going to be cooking in another curriculum area, explore instructional texts and produce a writing frame for recipes.

- After constructing writing frames during the literacy hour and applying them in other curriculum areas, remove the scaffolding provided by the frame and allow children to write in that style without the frame.

Lliteracy and other curriculum areas

Applying skills, knowledge and strategies acquired during the literacy hour in other curriculum areas provides real purposes and audiences. It also reinforces what the children have learned.

Exploit opportunities to write across the curriculum. For example ask children to

- make notes during a visitor's presentation

- write a report of a science investigation

- write a newspaper report about a local issue

- produce instructions for completing a model in design and technology

- write a diary account of life as an evacuee

- locate information during an historical enquiry

- write a guidebook for a local tourist attraction.

Time constraints do not allow for the production of extended pieces of writing during the literacy hour. Children can therefore generate extended pieces of writing during other curriculum areas.

Creating an appropriate classroom environment

The challenge facing children is great as they try to come to grips with the content, structure and style of the text, not to mention grammar, spelling and punctuation.

Your classroom environment can go a long way to support children in this process.

- Help children feel safe in taking risks by valuing all children's efforts.

- Encourage a problem-solving approach. Ask them to construct their own rules about the text type and to modify and extend these rules in light of their experience.

Display

Display a large A3 copy of the framework of the genre being learned for children to refer to, for example provide a photocopy of a relevant frame from this resource. This will support their independent writing by reminding them of the features of the text.

Display a list of the features of the chosen text type.

Resources

Make sure that you provide a variety of resources in the classroom. Use a copy of the frame on an OHT for whole class work. Provide a print-rich environment. This should include quality examples of a range of texts to provide good models for the children.

Value writing frames that have been written by yourself and the children by laminating them and keeping them easily available. Encourage children to refer to these frames when deciding on an appropriate text form for their independent writing.

Use writing frames as one of a range of supports including dictionaries, word banks, editing cards and proofreading prompts, thesauruses, key word and topic word lists.

And finally...

Writing Frames Made Easy aims to support teachers in making writing both purposeful and pleasurable for all children. Writing frames can provide the necessary scaffolding for children to develop into confident and independent writers.

Recount

Purpose of recount

Recount retells events. It develops alongside speech from a very early stage and is one of the fundamental communication skills – it is as old as humanity itself. As they move into Key Stage 1 children readily take to writing down their stories – it is a natural progression from years of verbally sharing the experiences of their own lives.

Text structure of recount

There are three elements to a recount.

- Orientation is the opening part, the scene setting in which key information about people and places is given. This prepares the reader for what is to come.

- Events are then retold in the order that they occurred and give the recount a sequence that allows the reader to follow the recount.

- Reorientation is the closing statement. It rounds things off, sums up events and draws the telling to a close.

Language features of recount

The language of recount has the following features.

- Events are told in the past tense.

- Events are told in chronological order.

- Connectives are time related, for example 'then', 'next' and 'after'.

- Focus is on individual or group participants, for example 'we did this' and 'I went first'.

Recount in the National Literacy Strategy

Here are two examples to illustrate how recount develops through the National Literacy Strategy.

- Year 1 Term 3 non-fiction 20 'to write simple recounts linked to topics of interest/study or to personal experience'. This includes topics such as retelling the events of a day trip and a visit to school by a fire engine.

- Year 3 Term 3 non-fiction 22 'experiment with recounting the same event in a variety of ways'. This includes topics such as writing a newspaper report on a netball match and describing it in a letter to a friend.

Everyday uses of recount

Children are already familiar with the structure of recount through television drama where stories of everyday life are retold by the characters. Written recounts are also widely available. For example, they are found in

- newspaper reports

- autobiographies (Roald Dahl's *Boy* is a good example)

- personal letters, postcards and email.

Teaching recount

When you teach recount don't forget its origins in the spoken word. The following are good examples of spoken word activities to use to help the development of recount.

- Sharing news is a powerful way to learn the structures of this genre.

- Drama and role-play provide speaking and listening opportunities for the whole class and allow children to experiment with experiences they have not had themselves.

- Telephone conversations conducted in the privacy of a home corner allow further development of recount skills.

When children come to writing down their verbal recounts the words are already there – they have been formed into an appropriate structure and therefore make the transition onto paper smoothly.

Value of recount to children

Verbal recount allows children to partake in the rich diversity that is human culture and tradition. Everyone has his or her tale to tell and children learn a great deal about relating to other people through sharing experiences.

Formalising recount in writing opens up a world beyond the immediate and present audience and allows children to communicate across space and time. A letter or an email forms a bridge between the child's world and the rest of the world.

Case study

Teaching objectives

Year 1 Term 3 non-fiction 18 'to read recounts and begin to recognise generic structure, e.g. ordered sequence of events, use of words like *first*, *next*, *after*, *when*'.

Year 1 Term 3 non-fiction 20 'to write simple recounts linked to topics of interest/study or to personal experience'.

The lesson

Working with a mixed Year 1/Year 2 class the teacher planned a topic on 'ourselves'. This gave lots of opportunities for the use of recount as a way of sharing news and recording aspects of the children's lives.

During shared reading the children read extracts from the big book of *My Holiday Diary*, which is in the Heinemann Discovery World Series. It is varied in structure and complexity and allows children with a range of abilities to work on the same text.

During guided reading the teacher used small versions of the same book. The Year 1 children concentrated on reading short excerpts, which gave a daily record of the family's holiday.

During shared writing the teacher wrote a recount of a day trip that her family had recently enjoyed. She asked the children to identify the key words of a recount such as 'then', 'next' and 'after'. These key words, which linked to the next statement, were underlined.

During individual work the Year 1 children wrote simple sentences on their writing frame to record a recent event in the life of their family, whilst Year 2 children did independent writing related to the topic.

During the plenary the teacher took one child's writing and copied it onto her flip chart. She asked the children to identify the elements that made it a recount and underlined these to reinforce the key features.

Use of writing frames

The writing frame used here was very basic and simply helped the writer record the events of the day. Space was allowed for an illustration as this helped formulate the writing.

Date _____

> A drawing of my story
>
>
>
>
>
>
> My story
> _____
>
> _____
>
> _____
>
> _____
>
> _____
>
> _____

Good words: next   then   after

Date _Monday   19th   June_

> A drawing of my story
>
> My story
> One morning I woke up.
>
> Then I jumpt on my mums and
>
> dads bed. They waket up. Next
>
> I ask them if I can go to the toy
>
> museum. They said "Yes". So I went
>
> the very next day.

Good words: next   then   after

Report

Purpose of report

A report describes the way things are. It is centred on a subject and is based on research. Reports should not be confused with recounts. This distinction needs to be made clear as it can be confusing when children are told, for instance, that a sports report is actually a recount. Children write a report by gathering information in note form from various sources before putting these into report form.

Text structure of report

There are two elements to a report.

- The opening consists of a general classification. This is the introduction and identifies the focus of the report, for example 'volcanoes are a natural phenomenon'. The opening may go on to become more technical depending on the year of the group involved, for example 'the badger (*Meles meles*) is a mammal in the Mustelidae family'.

- The main body of the text consists of a description. This is detailed, specific and can be divided with sub-headings such as 'qualities', 'parts', 'habits' and 'behaviour'.

Language features of report

The language of report has four main features. Reports

- are written in the present tense, for example 'volcanoes erupt and pour out lava'

- are non-chronological

- use sub-headings to break up the text into blocks of information

- can be read non-sequentially.

Report in the National Literacy Strategy

Report writing develops in a structured way as it moves through the Framework for teaching. Here are two examples.

- Year 2 Term 3 non-fiction 19 'to make simple notes from non-fiction texts, e.g. key words and phrases, page references, headings, to use in subsequent writing'. Here children are just beginning to develop their note making skills.

- Year 4 Term 1 non-fiction 27 'to write a non-chronological report, including the use of organisational devices, e.g. numbered lists, headings for conciseness'. Now children are learning to organise their notes in a more structured way.

Everyday uses of report

Reports present information on a wide variety of topics. Encourage children to see why we need information to make everyday decisions, for example

- health leaflets help us to self-diagnose a complaint

- car magazines help us choose which model of car we want to buy

- travel guides help us choose a holiday destination.

Teaching report

The most important point is to make clear the distinction between recount and report.

Introduce report writing by giving children a subject to research and on which to write a report. Allow them to underline information in different coloured pencils on a photocopy of a non-fiction text. Provide a key showing what categories of information the colours represent. Then group the information and give sub-headings as a way of structuring the finished piece.

Report writing provides a good opportunity to link to history, geography or science. Making this link not only helps develop report writing skills, it also helps children gain independence in learning in these areas.

Value of report to children

Writing a report allows a child to pursue an interest with satisfaction. It encourages them to gather information from a variety of sources and to decide on an accessible format in which to present the information to others. This is the beginning of research and prepares children for the decision making that is involved in later writing. It allows them to answer the following questions. What is important? What is marginal? What goes in? What is left out?

Case study

Teaching objectives

Year 5 Term 2 non-fiction 17 'to locate information confidently and efficiently'.

Year 5 Term 2 non-fiction 22 'to plan, compose, edit and refine short non-chronological reports'.

The lesson

The class was studying the ancient Greeks and the teacher used this as an opportunity to develop the children's research and report writing skills.

During shared reading they visited the school library. Here they reviewed the skills they needed to locate information books using the reference system and gathered a small selection of books. The teacher then modelled the skills needed to find specific information using the contents and index pages.

During shared writing the children were introduced to underlining text as a research technique and practised this on photocopies of a page from an information book.

The children were given different topics on the life of ancient Greece to research. They went away and worked in pairs to underline information relevant to their topic. The next stage was to generate and answer questions from their text using the writing frame.

During guided writing the teacher worked with a lower ability group to ensure they were using a range of questioning strategies.

During individual work the children went on to write their own reports.

During the plenary these reports were shared with other children.

Use of writing frames

The writing frame used allowed the children to generate questions once they had read a text. They recorded the answers to those questions before developing their writing into a more structured report format.

Questions and Answers

Use this sheet to record questions that can be answered by the text

1 Q

  A

2 Q

  A

3 Q

  A

4 Q

  A

Sub-headings

Group your questions into paragraphs.
Put the number of the question under the sub-heading it goes with.

_____ _____ _____

Greek City States

Greek city states were just like small countries with one large town. They often fought with each other, usually to get each others land. Each city state was called a 'polis'. (From this word we get 'politics' and 'police'.)

Athens was unusual because important decisions were made by a meeting of all the adult free men. This was the beginning of the democratic system. Other city city states were ruled by a tyrant. This was a man who ruled by force.

Most city states had houses and temples crowded into narrow streets. Athens was by far the biggest of all the states, and had many fine buildings. It was surrounded by a high wall to keep out enemies.

Explanation

Purpose of explanation

The purpose of explanation is to make clear the processes involved in natural and social phenomena, to explain how something works and to account for actions. Explanation is a writing technique that enables children to access learning in other curriculum areas such as science and geography and thus presents opportunities for literacy skill development outside the literacy hour. There are many opportunities in the QCA schemes of work to make these all-important links.

Text structure of explanation

There are three elements to explanation.

- The introduction to the explanation is a general statement, for example 'the heart is a pump'.

- A series of logical steps explain how or why something occurs, for example 'as the muscles of the heart contract blood is pumped through arteries'.

- These steps continue until the final stage is reached and the explanation is complete.

Language features of explanation

The language of explanation has three main features.

- It is generally written in simple present tense.

- It uses time connectives, for example 'then' and 'next'.

- It uses causal connectives, for example 'because', 'so' and 'this causes'.

Explanation in the National Literacy Strategy

Here are two examples of how explanation writing develops through the Framework.

- Year 2 Term 2 non-fiction 21 'to produce simple flow charts or diagrams that explain a process'. Here children use visual techniques to begin the process of ordering information necessary for an explanation.

- Year 4 Term 2 non-fiction 24 'to improve the cohesion of written explanations through paragraphing and the use of link phrases and organisational devices such as

sub-headings and numbering'. Now explanation giving is more involved and enables children to experience greater complexity in communicating their findings in other curriculum areas such as science.

Everyday uses of explanation

Make explanation sources available for children to read in your classroom, for example

- posters that illustrate scientific processes such as the water cycle

- leaflets that detail health issues and explain biological processes

- encyclopaedia entries that deal with geographical or historical events.

Teaching explanation

Link explanation to other curriculum areas. Teach and refine the text structure and language features of explanation during the literacy hour then practise during work in other areas. This gives opportunities for extended writing.

For example, during practical work in science you may grow a plant from seed and explain to the class the processes involved, such as water absorption and photosynthesis. Follow up the experimental work and class discussion with a piece of extended writing detailing these processes. This helps learning in both literacy and science.

Value of explanation to children

By developing the skills of explanation children understand more fully the processes involved in the phenomena they are studying. They learn to relate their knowledge and understanding to other people in a coherent form which is readily accessible.

These skills are particularly useful as children move on with the curriculum in the sciences.

Teaching objectives

Year 5 Term 2 non-fiction 'to read a range of explanatory texts, investigating and noting features of impersonal style'.

Case study

Year 5 Term 2 non-fiction 22 'to plan, compose, edit and refine short non-chronological reports and explanatory texts'.

The lesson

The class was familiar with the organisation of the school reference library and children were able to locate information confidently. The teacher built on these skills and used health leaflets obtained from the local surgery.

During shared reading the children looked at a range of health leaflets covering the workings of the heart and lungs and how these organs can be damaged by people's choice of lifestyle. Reading the leaflets informed the children of the issues and gave them valuable information in the form of labelled diagrams, which would be helpful in their explanation writing.

During shared writing the teacher modelled the writing frame that she wanted the children to use in order to gather information from leaflets and reference books. She also took the opportunity to inform the children of the structure of a piece of explanatory text.

During individual work the children researched their subject, gathered information from leaflets and books and made notes.

During the plenary children worked in small groups to share their notes before making a brief presentation to the class on the workings of the organ they had been given to study.

Outside the literacy hour children needed time to organise their notes and present them in a completed form. This happened at a different time to the skills teaching and note making.

Use of writing frames

The writing frame shown here was to help children organise their note making in a way that helped their writing develop into a finished piece. By Year 5 many children are able to design their own writing frames for the finished piece or even manage without them if the preparatory work has been done on a planning writing frame.

Notes for an explanation

Subject

General statement

Key facts
-
-
-
-
-

Scientific words

Conclusion

The lungs

Your lungs are a bit like big bags that fit inside your rib cage. They are connected to your wind pipe which ends at your nose and mouth! When you take a breath, the air goes down the wind pipe into your lungs. Normally you would take a big breath and your lungs would have to expand to let all the air in! If you smoke, all the chemicals in the tobacco, especially tar, would go straight down to the lungs and will give you lung cancer.

Tar is used for making brand new roads. The worst part is, Tar is very addictive so once you start you can't stop. Which means you slowly die as your lungs fill up.

Instruction

Purpose of instruction

Instruction guides the reader to do something through a series of sequenced steps. Following written instructions helps teach young children the value of learning to read. Suddenly they become aware that – with written instructions in their hands – they can do something without someone having to tell them how. It also means they can direct the activities of others in the same way.

Text structure of instruction

Instructions have the following structure.

- They open with a goal, or a statement of what is to be achieved, for example 'how to programme a video recorder'.

- Next the materials and equipment needed are recorded.

- Then sequential steps to achieve the goal are given.

- Often there is a diagram or illustration to help make the instructions clearer.

Language features of instruction

Instruction has the following language features.

- It is written in the imperative, for example 'first you turn on the video recorder' or 'turn on the video recorder'.

- It is written in chronological order using words such as 'first', 'next' and 'after that'.

- It uses generalised human agents rather than named individuals.

Instruction in the National Literacy Strategy

Here are two examples to illustrate how instruction writing develops through the Framework.

- Year 3 Term 2 non-fiction 16 'to write instructions, e.g. rules for playing games, recipes, using a range of organisational devices, e.g. lists, dashes, commas for lists in sentences, recognising the importance of correct sequence'. This skill develops quickly from simple instruction writing in Year 2.

- Year 5 Term 1 non-fiction 25 'to write instructional texts, and test them out, e.g. instructions for loading computers, design briefs for technology, rules for games'. This is advanced instruction writing and involves text as well as numbered points. The text is tried out, evaluated and modified.

Everyday uses of instruction

Instructions are everywhere. They are in

- recipe books
- computer software handbooks
- construction kit handbooks.

Teaching instruction

Introduce instruction writing by asking children to bring in from home examples such as a recipe on the back of a cereal box or assembly instructions for a toy. Study these through shared and guided reading so children become familiar with the text conventions. Modelling the writing of instructions in shared and guided writing is an effective way to teach instruction conventions.

When they are familiar with the text conventions ask them to write some instructions of their own. These are best written about a process in which the children are engaged. For example, get them to write instructions for making a sandwich or constructing a model.

Children's use of this genre also benefits from the development of skills outside the literacy hour.

Value of instruction to children

Children benefit in two ways from learning to use instruction. First, it teaches them to read and follow instructions – this gives them a sense of freedom from having to be told how to do something. Second, they learn how to instruct other people in writing, in a logical and structured way. The reader is then able to repeat the activity by following the instructions.

Case study

Teaching objectives

Year 3 Term 2 non-fiction 12 'to identify the different purposes of instructional text'.

Year 3 Term 2 non-fiction 16 'to write instructions, e.g. rules for playing a game, recipes, using a range of organisational devices and recognising the importance of correct sequence'.

The lesson

The class worked in food technology to learn about healthy choices. In the literacy hour they investigated different forms of instruction giving before writing up their own procedures for making a healthy sandwich.

For preparatory work the children gathered from home a collection of instructions for different everyday processes. These included recipes, game rules and instructions to programme a video recorder.

During shared reading the children read out to the class the lists of instructions they had gathered from home. The teacher had enlarged several lists of instructions and displayed these for the class to read together. They then went on to discuss the features and layout of lists of instructions.

During shared writing the teacher modelled writing lists of instructions for preparing several simple foods and drinks, for example beans on toast and a cup of tea. As he did this he talked about the features the children had already identified from reading.

During individual work the children used the writing frame to write out their own numbered lists to describe the steps they would take to make a healthy and delicious sandwich.

The children then took a break from their literacy work to make their sandwiches and then came back together to eat them and evaluate them. They discussed their preferences and wrote a sentence to describe how their sandwich tasted.

Use of writing frames

The writing frame used here starts with a space for the children to record their ingredients in a list. It concludes with a box to write a sentence describing the taste of the sandwich and a box to suggest any improvements that could be made. The body of the frame is for the numbered list of instructions.

Title	_____
Ingredients	____ ____ ____
	____ ____ ____

Instructions

Describe how your sandwich tasted.

How would you improve your sandwich?

Title	Instructions for making a sandwich
Ingredients	____ ____ ____
	____ ____ ____

Instructions

1. Choose a bread roll and filling's to go inside it. If you are having butter in it then make sure that it isn't too fattening.

2. Cut the bread roll long ways.

3. Put your fittings in side the roll.

4. Put salami into the roll but make sure that you don't put it in too thick.

5. Then put some salad in it.

6. Then eat it !!!.

Describe how your sandwich tasted.

How would you improve your sandwich?

Persuasion and discussion

Purpose of persuasion and discussion

Persuasion and discussion could be two separate genres. However, in the context of class teaching within the Framework you use similar strategies to teach both. Persuasion is arguing the case for a point of view whereas discussion involves presenting arguments and information from differing viewpoints not necessarily your own.

Text structure of persuasion and discussion

Persuasion contains the following elements.

- The thesis is an opening statement and makes clear the point being put forward.

- Arguments are reasons to support the thesis.

- Reiteration is the process of summarising and restating the opening position and acts as a conclusion.

Discussion contains the following elements.

- There is a statement of the issue and a preview of the main arguments.

- There are arguments for and against the case with supporting evidence.

- There is a recommendation, which is the point of view put forward as a conclusion to the gathering and weighing of evidence.

Language features of persuasion and discussion

Persuasion and discussion share the same language features.

- They are written in the present tense.

- There is a clear sequential pathway.

- Connectives support the logical development of the case, for example 'this shows', 'however' and 'because'.

Persuasion and discussion in the National Literacy Strategy

The following examples show how persuasion and discussion develop through the National Literacy Strategy.

- Year 4 Term 3 non-fiction 21 'to assemble and sequence points in order to plan the presentation of a point of view'. Adopting a point of view and supporting it is vital for future work.

- Year 5 Term 3 non-fiction 19 'to construct an argument in note form or full text to persuade others of a point of view'. Earlier work on adopting a point of view is now developed more fully.

Everyday uses of persuasion and discussion

There are some excellent real examples from which children can learn, for example

- letters columns in local papers

- for and against articles in newspapers and magazines

- leaflets from campaigning groups.

Teaching persuasion and discussion

Whether complex or simple, the issues dealt with should be real. Allow children to cut their teeth on safe school arguments such as whether to only allow the eating of fruit as a breaktime snack. Move on to a local issue such as the building of a hotel on a nearby patch of wasteland. By the end of Year 6 discuss more controversial issues such as passive smoking and vegetarianism.

Allow plenty of opportunity to gather information on the issues as stimulus for structured class discussion. Discussion allows views to begin to develop before moving on to open debate. Ask the children to put together the points they have discussed to produce a letter or a short article for the local paper or a national campaign.

Value of persuasion and discussion to children

Constructive argument is perhaps one of the least developed communication skills in our society! Many of us simply don't know how to present our case or don't understand the position of someone with whom we disagree. When children develop these skills in their primary years it allows them to become effective debaters who can contribute in a positive way to the development of their society. It also allows children to develop confidence and learn how to manage conflict.

pfp © pfp 2001 ISBN 1 874050 79 1 pfp, 61 Gray's Inn Road, London WC1X 8TH May be photocopied for use within the purchasing institution only.

Case study

Teaching objectives

Year 5 Term 3 non-fiction 12 'to read and evaluate letters, eg. from newspapers'.

Year 5 Term 3 non-fiction 17 'to draft or write individual, group and class letters for real purposes, eg. put a point of view, comment on an emotive issue, protest'.

The lesson

Having worked through a series of lessons on the issue of passive smoking linked to science and PSHE the children were ready to produce a letter of protest on the issue.

During shared reading they looked at letters to the editor in the local newspaper. These were enlarged and annotated in class to highlight the features of an effective letter.

During shared writing the children began to map out the shape of a letter to a local restaurant complaining about smoking. They took each of the elements they had discovered and discussed its part in the letter.

During group work the children discussed the form their letter would take, shared the planning of the letter and wrote their own individual letters using the writing frame. They discussed these and edited them together.

During the plenary letters were shared with the class and improvements were discussed.

During follow up the children did more non-fiction writing in the form of information leaflets and posters. This formed part of an integrated topic with the literacy elements being covered in detail during the literacy hour and other elements being covered outside of it.

Use of writing frames

The writing frame used here was generated by the children during discussions that took place in the shared writing session of the literacy hour. Children could have been given a pre-designed writing frame, but by Year 5 they are increasingly able to create their own with the support of their teachers and peers.

| Your address |
| Date |

Dear

Introduce yourself

Make your point and back it up

Offer a solution

Sign off politely

The Minster School
Enwell Street
Warminster
BA12 8JA

19th January 2000

Dear Sir/Madam,

I am writing to say that earlier this week I came into your restaurant and had a meal with my family. I really enjoyed it but it was spoilt by a couple of smokers.

My first complaint is that passive smoking can cause cancer and give germs - which is not good for young children or babies. Secondly when I got home I smelt really awful and my eyes stung a bit. Also for people with asthma it really doesn't help at all.

To solve these problems you could check the air conditioning works, or have a non-smoking area built, maybe in the garden (if you have one). Whatever way, I'd really like something done about it. If you can't do any of my suggestions please could you provide me and any non-smokers with gas masks so I can come and enjoy your meals without smokers.

yours faithfully
Scott Warrington

Poetry

Purpose of poetry

Poetry is concerned with the emotional and imaginative description of the world and is a tantalisingly difficult medium for children to work with. It is the closest writing comes to being an artform and in encouraging children to develop as poets this needs to be recognised. It is a form of writing that allows children to explore their feelings and relationships with other people and the world around them.

Text structure of poetry

Text structures in poems are many and varied but here are some common features.

- The text is often written in short lines.
- Lines may be grouped together into verses to highlight themes in the poem.
- The last words of some lines, such as those that are consecutive or alternate, may rhyme.

Language features of poetry

Poetry often has the following features.

- It is written in imaginative and descriptive language with a high use of adjectives.
- The use of simile and metaphor to emphasise pictorial imagery.
- Poetry is often allegorical (the meaning is presented symbolically).

Poetry in the National Literacy Strategy

The Framework for teaching gives many objectives aimed at developing the skills of reading and writing poetry. These need to be taught as systematically as any other literacy skill. Objectives in the word and sentence level sections are also useful as they form the building blocks of poems. These objectives do, however, only teach the structure. Work on poetry benefits from being linked to work in the arts as a way of drawing out emotional and imaginative responses. Here are two examples of how poetry writing is developed in the Framework.

- Year 2 Term 3 fiction and poetry 11 'to use humorous verse as a structure for children to write their own by adaptation, mimicry or substitution'.

- Year 4 Term 1 fiction and poetry 14 'to write poems based on personal or imagined experience, linked to poems read'.

Everyday uses of poetry

When you present children with poetry in the classroom environment offer as great a diversity as possible. This helps them appreciate the varied nature of the poetic form. For example, offer

- nursery rhymes with predictable and repeating patterns
- themed poetry collections, for example on animals or summer
- humorous and nonsense poems
- tongue-twisters and riddles
- alliterative poems.

Teaching poetry

Immerse the children in poetry from the outset and give them every opportunity to read and be read to. Share and discuss poetry as a class and make sure you have a varied collection in your book corner. This way, when they come to write poetry for themselves they will have plenty of models on which to base their work.

Writing frames are useful in the brainstorming stage of poetry writing when children are gathering their thoughts in preparation for organising the structure of the poem. The format of a frame allows children to record their feelings in a meaningful way. As they develop as writers this scaffolding is gradually removed until they are able to cope with a blank piece of paper.

Value of poetry to children

For some, poetry is an undervalued form and it is in need of a renaissance. Young children love the way poetic text rolls around the mouth when spoken aloud and they need every encouragement to take this enjoyment into their writing. Poetry lifts the soul and a child who is able to carry their love of poetry into adult life will treasure it. There can be many layers of meaning within a poem, which can bring a greater understanding to the way in which people see themselves as individuals and as a part of society.

Case study

Teaching objectives

Year 3 Term 3 fiction and poetry 7 'to select, prepare, read aloud and recite by heart poetry that plays with language or entertains; to recognise rhyme, alliteration and other patterns of sound that create effects'.

Year 3 Term 3 fiction and poetry 15 'to write poetry that uses sound to create effects, eg. onomatopoeia, alliteration, distinctive rhythms'.

The lesson

The teacher had been working at building self-esteem and developing good/positive relationships within her class and had used stories and poems from different cultures as a way of helping the children celebrate differences. The class settled on Grace Nichols as a favourite poet.

During shared reading the teacher photocopied on to acetate the poem 'Morning' from Grace Nichols' book *Give Yourself a Hug* and displayed it using an overhead projector. The children read the poem and learnt it by heart. They discussed the patterns within the poem and were able to see how these patterns helped them to remember the words.

During shared writing the children sat in a circle and contributed their thoughts on their own experiences of morning in their homes. The teacher scribed these for them as she sat in the middle with a large sheet of paper. This was then displayed as a class brainstorm.

Working in pairs the children completed the writing frame to record what the morning was like for them. They then took each thought and turned it into a line for their poem.

During individual work the children wrote their own poem following the pattern and rhythm of the original but inserting their own experiences.

During the plenary the class recited their poetry.

Use of writing frames

The writing frame used here was for planning purposes rather than for writing the final draft of the poem. The frame allowed the children to record their thoughts and feelings on the theme as a brainstorm before reordering them and drafting them into a poem.

Poetry Brainstorm

| Sounds | Smells |
| Sights | Feelings |

Try out your ideas for a first line here

Morning

Morning comes with my kettle singing

Morning comes with my dog barking

Morning comes with the door bell ringing

Morning comes with the tap running

Morning comes with the letters dropping

Morning comes with my sister shaking me

Morning comes with my mum pulling me out of bed

Rebecca Rowe   year 5

Narrative

Purpose of narrative

The narrative form is as old as language itself and has given us tales of great wonder and joy, sadness and horror. It is the most versatile of forms and strikes a chord deep within us. A tale well told takes us anywhere in this world or out of it and to any time past, present or future – it convinces us that we are right there, right now.

Text structure of narrative

The basic text structure has a beginning, a middle and an end that tells the tale as a sequence of events. Narratives

- are generally told in the first or third person
- describe characters and settings to help the plot develop
- may raise questions or problems at various points in the plot and resolve them later.

Language features of narrative

Narrative has the following features.

- It uses sequential language common to recount and narrative, such as 'first', 'then', 'next' and 'after'.
- It uses direct and reported speech.
- It has complex sentence structure.
- It uses a variety of word classes.

Narrative in the National Literacy Strategy

The Framework for teaching sets out to cover the entire range of narrative skills appropriate to a primary child. By the end of Year 6 children are much more aware of the range and scope of a story, the depths they can go to and the many levels at which they can work. A richly complex story is now within the grasp of every child. Here are a couple of examples.

- Year 1 Term 1 fiction and poetry 11 'to make simple picture storybooks with sentences'.
- Year 3 Term 2 fiction and poetry 10 'to write alternative sequels to traditional stories using the same characters and settings'.

Everyday uses of narrative

Narrative is the most prolific form of literature. Ensure children have access to a variety of narrative genres, for example

- stories of everyday life
- stories of heroism and adventure
- stories with mythological characters
- stories about animals
- stories set in other places or times.

Teaching narrative

As with poetry the value of writing frames to narrative lies in the planning or brainstorming stages. Well-planned frames allow children to create characters and settings for their stories. The plot structure that is so important to a good tale can be worked out in advance on a frame. Specific elements that you want the children to develop, such as more adventurous adjectives or cleverly used adverbs, are included in this planning stage. When they come to write the story they will have done what all good writers of fiction do – prepared the ground.

Value of narrative to children

Narrative is not only entertaining. By allowing children to share in the lives of people in other places and other times it helps them relate to other experiences – to live them and learn from them. Narrative allows children to find role models and to develop as people.

Writing stories for themselves allows children to express their feelings and thoughts through the characters they create. This helps them understand and gain control over their own experiences.

Stories form bridges between cultures and in a multicultural country it is important that children of all nationalities and faiths share each other's traditional tales in the name of mutual understanding and respect.

© pfp 2001 ISBN 1 874050 79 1   pfp, 61 Gray's Inn Road, London WC1X 8TH May be photocopied for use within the purchasing institution only.

Case study

Teaching Objectives

Year 2 Term 2 fiction and poetry 6 'to identify and describe characters, expressing own views and using words and phrases from texts'.

Year 2 Term 2 fiction and poetry 14 'to write character profiles, e.g. simple descriptions, posters, passports, using key words and phrases that describe or are spoken by characters in the text'.

The lesson

The class had been using traditional stories as a basis for building character profiles, settings and plot structure.

During shared reading the teacher used a big book of *The Three Billy Goats Gruff* and read the story with the children. They read the whole story through first and then discussed different elements.

During shared writing they began to build up a profile of the troll. They discussed his appearance, personality, likes and dislikes. They discussed his home and what he ate. The teacher recorded the children's comments as single words or short descriptive phrases on a large sheet of paper under sub-headings.

During individual work the majority of the class completed the writing frame to illustrate and describe the troll.

During guided writing the teacher worked with a lower ability group and helped them complete a larger copy of the writing frame.

During the plenary the children were paired and asked to compare each other's character illustrations and written descriptions to see how closely the two matched.

During follow up work the children created character descriptions for their own characters using the same writing frame. They created settings and story plots and finally wrote their own stories in the style of a traditional tale.

Use of writing frames

The writing frame used here was designed by the teacher as a way of giving her children the freedom from worry that a blank piece of paper can create. Placing the illustration at the beginning of the frame helped children to develop their written descriptions.

Name _____ Title _____

What they look like

_____
_____
_____
_____

Their personality

_____
_____
_____
_____

Their hobbies

_____
_____
_____

Name _Alex Smith_ Title _The Troll_

What they look like

He's got red eyes, brown hair and he's purple. He has a horn hat, long teeth and a rag shirt.

Their personality

He is mean, cross and very hungry and loud and angry.

Their hobbies

Eating goats and climbing on the bridg.

© pfp 2001 ISBN 1 874050 79 1 pfp, 61 Gray's Inn Road, London WC1X 8TH May be photocopied for use within the purchasing institution only.

Using writing frames in Key Stage 1

Introduction

This stand-alone section for Key Stage 1 provides a range of ready-to-use photocopiable writing frames supported by teachers' notes. These sheets provide additional suggestions for meeting the needs of all children. There are examples of differentiated and cross-curricular writing frames. These curriculum links are identified in the Key Stage 1 links table on page 28.

The frames can be used as a starting point when introducing a new text type. They provide models of the various features of different text types which can be adapted to meet the needs of the children.

When used as a teaching tool, rather than as photocopiable worksheets, they will contribute to the learning process and will support children in becoming independent writers. Once children are familiar with the text form and are confident, the frame can be removed, leaving the children able to write imaginatively and with creativity.

The case studies given on pages 12 and 24 demonstrate how to use writing frames effectively in Key Stage 1 classes. Additional guidance is also given overleaf.

Summary of teaching guidance provided on pages 5–10

Writing frames support the development of children's independent writing. They direct children's attention to features of different texts. These include purpose and audience, structure and layout, grammar, punctuation and vocabulary.

Writing frames can challenge children to widen their writing experiences. They can support writing within a new genre, especially for children who are experiencing difficulty in developing or sustaining an aspect of writing. Careful assessment of children's independent writing will indicate whether a child would benefit from using a writing frame and if so, with what aspects of writing they need support.

During the literacy hour, writing frames can be generated on paper or on the computer. They can be created and completed by the teacher, jointly between the teacher and children and collaboratively by children and their peers.

To get the most out of writing frames, teachers need to share good quality texts with their children and use these as a model for children's writing. This writing needs to have a real purpose that children understand, for example by exploiting links with other

curriculum areas. Children also need to write for real audiences, for example their peers, younger and older children, parents, visitors and the local community.

The teacher's role is to explicitly teach the features of different texts and then model the writing process. Both fiction and non-fiction texts should be used for shared, guided and independent work. Children also need to be given adequate time to practice and reinforce their writing skills, both within the literacy hour and in other curriculum areas. The literacy hour should be seen as a workshop in which children acquire literacy skills that can then be applied across the curriculum.

Teachers can support the use of writing frames by encouraging and valuing children's attempts. A stimulating, print-rich environment should be provided. This would contain many examples of different text types and resources to support the writing process such as dictionaries, word banks, editing cards, proofreading prompts, thesauruses, key word lists and topic word lists. An enlarged copy of the writing frame can also be displayed to support children's independent writing.

Using writing frames in nursery and Reception classes

Early years teachers are powerful models for young children. Children copy what they see teachers doing, including reading and writing. Teachers can exploit this to jointly produce simple writing frames that can be completed by the children. When using writing frames with very young children the emphasis is on shared and modelled writing. The children are not expected to create or complete writing frames independently.

As the aim is for children to develop into confident readers and writers, it is important that teachers demonstrate their own enthusiasm and pleasure. Provide opportunities throughout the day for shared, modelled and guided reading and writing. During these sessions, encourage the children to talk about their own 'reading' and 'writing'. Following these sessions, encourage children to try writing their own texts or act as scribe for them.

Share good books, both fiction and non-fiction, with children. Look for opportunities to identify and discuss their specific features including the use of headings, titles, diagrams and illustrations. Look for interesting vocabulary and letter patterns, rhyming words and familiar vocabulary.

Let children see you writing for yourself as well as for them. Let them know why you are writing and for whom you are writing. When producing shared writing, include the features

and language of books that you have read together. Encourage the children to contribute and accept their suggestions. During these shared sessions you can produce simple writing frames that include the basic structures of the texts that you are reading together. The writing frames themselves can become shared reading texts and can be made available in various writing situations.

Provide opportunities for children to 'write for fun' within play situations and at a writing table. Your role-play area could become the vet's, a shop, a doctor's surgery or a travel agency. Whatever the setting, provide appropriate texts to refer to and materials to write in role. These opportunities may include order forms, receipts, posters, adverts, prescriptions, booking forms, brochures, messages and lists. Simple writing frames can be provided for these and appropriate topic words could be displayed. You can also model how to use these writing forms by going into role yourself.

Young children will 'write' by making marks on the page. As their confidence grows, they will replicate both spoken and written phrases, particularly rhymes and songs. Make sure that you value and praise their endeavours. Demonstrate this by asking children to 'read' their 'writing' back to you and the class, by displaying their work for others to see and by responding positively to their attempts.

Using writing frames in Year 1

As children move through Year 1 they become increasingly familiar with a range of writing forms, both fiction and non-fiction, including stories, signs, cards, poems, lists, letters and messages. Their confidence in writing simple sentences grows and they want to share their writing with others. Encourage this in pairs and groups, during assemblies and with parents and visitors. Children will now demonstrate a willingness to write for their own interest and to experiment with new words. Continue to talk with children about their writing and to encourage them to write for themselves as well as for others.

Writing frames, used sensitively, can support Year 1 children in developing further as writers. Within the structure of the literacy

hour, the initial emphasis is going to be on shared, modelled and guided writing to teach text forms such as recounts, reports and instructions. Use these daily sessions to model the use of text features such as titles and contents pages. Continue to discuss the purpose and audience of the text and to identify the use of vocabulary, punctuation and sentence structure in different text types.

Writing frames can also be used to model new skills including producing simple plans before writing, making simple corrections and improvements and rereading writing to check for sense. When attempting a new text type, such as instructional writing, frames can support and challenge children in using unfamiliar sentence construction and linguistic features such as the use of imperative verbs at the beginning of a sentence. Use writing frames to extend children's use of connectives and subject-specific vocabulary.

Again, use writing frames within a stimulating and supportive environment. Build up a class word bank and model the use of this when writing. Set group and individual activities based on the shared, modelled and guided sessions. This will support children as they face the challenge of developing as writers.

Using writing frames in Year 2

Children in Year 2 are increasingly confident with a range of familiar text forms including recounts, stories and letters. They will be aware of some of the purposes of writing and will be familiar with basic sentence structures. Continue to provide real writing experiences such as letters, invitations, signs, instructions, lists and labels.

During shared reading sessions, encourage children to identify the features of effective texts and list these. Continue to use writing frames to focus on the purpose and audience of different text types and to develop children's control of sentence structure, text organisation and punctuation. Move from modelling the use of planning frames to encouraging children to complete their own. Continue to model simple editing and proofreading and jointly construct a prompt card to support children in their own early attempts. Model the use of this. Encourage children to suggest improvements to each other's writing.

Use writing frames to support children's use of varying connectives, sentence beginnings and structures. Draw on their growing experience of language. For example, a narrative writing frame may begin with 'Once upon a time...' Display collections of effective story beginnings and endings, good descriptions and new vocabulary as well as word banks. This will encourage independence.

Encourage children to consider what the reader needs to know and how best to write this. Model how to do this during shared, modelled and guided writing sessions. Continue to encourage children to reread their work to ensure that it makes sense.

Opportunities are still needed for practice and reinforcement, both during the literacy hour and across the curriculum and children should be encouraged to share their writing. Always praise their attempts.

And finally...

Writing frames have a great deal to offer the children of Key Stage 1. Using writing frames in Key Stage 1 will support children in taking risks. By breaking the writing process down into manageable stages, they enable children to focus on one aspect of their writing at a time. This will enable sustained writing and will motivate children by providing early success.

Working with the frames and lesson notes on offer here will set you firmly on the path to becoming a fan of these simple but effective tools. The next step is to go it alone. You will notice that not every objective in the Framework for teaching is covered here. Find one that isn't and be brave, give it a go, design your own writing frames and see how they work.

Key Stage 1 links table

Genre	Title	NLS Objective	QCA link	Page
Recount	**Shared experiences**	Year 1 Term 3 non-fiction 18, 20	Geography Unit 5	29
Report	**Questions and answers**	Year 1 Term 3 non-fiction 9, 22	History Units 2 and 3 ICT Unit 1b	33
Report	**Note making and report writing**	Year 2 Term 3 non-fiction 15, 16, 19, 20	Science Unit 2b	37
Explanation	**How it works**	Year 1 Term 3 non-fiction 17, 21	Science Unit 1e	41
Explanation	**Why it happened**	Year 2 Term 3 non-fiction 16, 20	History Unit 5	45
Instruction	**Writing simple instructions**	Year 2 Term 1 non-fiction 13, 15–18	Information Technology Unit 2d	49
Poetry	**Rhyming poetry**	Year 1 Term 1 fiction and poetry 6, 10	Information Technology Units 1a and 1b	53
Poetry	**Humorous verse**	Year 2 Term 3 fiction and poetry 6, 8, 11	Information Technology Units 2a and 2b	57
Narrative	**Story plotting**	Year 1 Term 2 fiction and poetry 4, 14	Geography Unit 1	61
Narrative	**Story settings**	Year 2 Term 1 fiction and poetry 5, 13	Geography Unit 6	65

© pfp 2001 ISBN 1 874050 79 1   pfp, 61 Gray's Inn Road, London WC1X 8TH May be photocopied for use within the purchasing institution only.

Shared experience

Recount

NLS Y1 T3 non-fiction 18, 20

QCA Geography Unit 5 Where in the world is Barnaby Bear? Recounts of real holidays and day trips lead into writing imaginary holidays that Barnaby has enjoyed and allows the development of recount skills into narrative skills.

Lesson notes

Start by using Frame 1 News Pictures. This allows the everyday practise of news sharing to become an opportunity to develop recount skills. Ask the children to describe a recent family event on the sheet using pictures and short sentences. Stress the need for events to be put in the order in which they occurred.

During shared reading ask some of the children to read out their accounts. Once a few have been shared ask the class to identify common strands. They will need some encouragement to see that the events happen in order and that certain key words are used – the realisation of these points is important and is worth emphasising. Once these strands have been identified use them as teaching points.

During shared writing write a recount of a trip you personally have enjoyed and emphasise the ordering of events. Underline key words such as 'first', 'next', 'after' and 'when' to highlight their important role in linking sentences.

During independent or group work use the writing frames as follows.

- Frame 2 News Sentences. This frame allows children to begin to turn their pictures and short sentences into more complex sentences – the prompt words supplied help them in this.

- Frame 3 My News Report. This frame allows children to write a whole piece of text and to illustrate it.

During guided writing work with your less able children to ensure they write simple sentences incorporating the key words supplied. With your more able children, work to come up with a list of other words that could be used in a recount.

During the plenary review those all-important few words that make a recount what it is and reinforce its sequential structure.

Teaching points

Develop speaking and listening skills by using role-play whenever possible during your work on recount. Telephone conversations in the home corner or sharing news while doing the shopping help to encourage the imaginative dimension in children's work.

Focus on sharing tales of travels – no matter how long or short. Put a large map of the country on your classroom wall and put in a map pin – with the child's name attached – every time someone visits a relative in another part of the country. Ask them to recount these events to the class.

Use a pack of prompt cards on which the words 'first', 'next', 'after' and 'when' are written. When sharing news ask the child speaking to make sure they use each of these words during their retelling.

Tape record recounts of a school trip and have the tape available for children to listen to, with a photograph album of the day, in your book corner. Children will enjoy reliving the day long after the event.

Involving parents

Show the children how much you value their news by inviting their parents in to describe – with their child – a family outing. It can be a shopping trip, a visit to the park or a trip to the seaside. Some of the accounts may be useful in the Barnaby Bear unit in the geography scheme of work and parents may be able to help with holiday mementos such as photographs and postcards.

Name .... **Date** ....

NEWS PICTURES

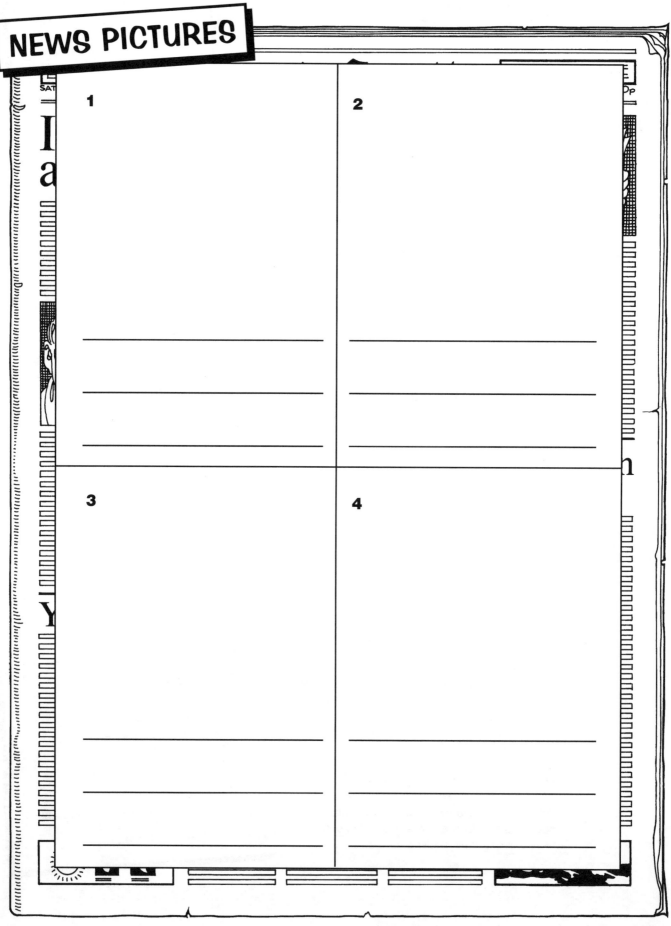

1

2

3

4

WRITING FRAMES MADE EASY • Shared experience • page 2 of 4

© pfp 2001 ISBN 1 874050 79 1 pfp, 61 Gray's Inn Road, London WC1X 8TH May be photocopied for use within the purchasing institution only.

Name ....   **Date** ....

NEWS SENTENCES

First _____

_____

Next _____

_____

Then _____

_____

After that _____

_____

When _____

_____

In the end _____

_____

Name ....   **Date** ....

MY NEWS REPORT

Put your title here _____

Put your picture here

Put your news here _____

_____

_____

_____

_____

_____

_____

Good words   *first, next, then, after, when*

© pfp 2001 ISBN 1 874050 79 1 pfp, 61 Gray's Inn Road, London WC1X 8TH May be photocopied for use within the purchasing institution only. pfp

Questions and answers

Report

NLS Y1 T3 non-fiction 9, 22

QCA History Unit 2 What were homes like long ago? What sorts of homes do people live in today?

History Unit 3 What were seaside holidays like in the past? What is different and the same about seaside holidays now and then?

Lesson notes

Before the lesson gather together resources that allow the children to read simple texts on the subject, look at photographs and handle artefacts. This gives a history focus to the subject and leads to the natural and instinctive urge of all six-year-olds to ask questions.

During shared reading use a big book or an enlarged photocopy of a page of text and read a piece about life in the past. Then examine any photographs and artefacts you have collected and discuss these different ways of finding out about the past.

During shared writing encourage the children to ask questions. Scribe for them and then ask them what they notice about the way a question is written. The use of words such as 'what', 'when', and 'why' and the use of question marks are your teaching points. Then discuss ways of finding answers, such as asking someone who knows, looking in a book or watching a TV programme.

During group work give groups of children a photograph or artefact to take away and discuss. Ask them to generate their own questions and go on to find answers before writing a short report.

Use the writing frames as follows.

- Frame 1 Writing Questions. This frame helps children generate a range of questions during group work thereby broadening their questioning vocabulary.

- Frame 2 Finding Answers. Use this frame for independent work once children have generated their questions. It encourages them to use more than one source to find answers.

- Frame 3 Report Writing. Use this frame for independent work once the children have gathered evidence. It allows them to put their questions and answers together to form simple sentences and, finally, to write a short report.

During the plenary look at photographs of the past and discuss with the children any clues they can see as to the way people used to live.

Teaching points

Find questions and answers in history programmes or television to help the children develop their skills in an enjoyable way. You could use Frame 1 Writing Questions before watching the programme and allow children to use Frame 2 Finding Answers as they view it.

Put up a question and answer display with a collection of pictures and artefacts from the past and questions about them. Attach a blank sheet of paper beneath each question to allow children to write answers to the questions. After a suitable period of display, discuss with the children each piece of evidence, the question and the various answers.

A further lesson in questions and answers can be gained if you dress up as a character from the historical period you are studying.

Do your research and allow the children to interview you. You can use the writing frames provided here for this.

 ICT

Using a word bank, Unit 1B in the QCA for ICT. During the short focused task introduce children to word banks and teach them to select words using a mouse. Create a word bank for the subject you are studying. In the integrated activity children can produce a short piece of text putting questions and answers into simple sentences using words from the bank. They can then practise saving and printing their work.

Name ....   **Date** ....

WRITING QUESTIONS

What _____

_____

When _____

_____
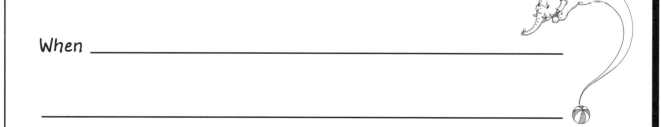

Who _____

_____
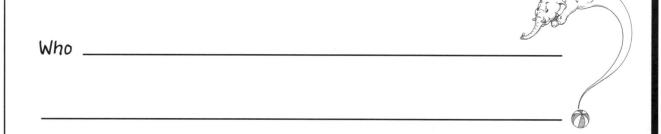

How _____

_____

WRITING FRAMES MADE EASY • Questions and answers • page 2 of 4

Name .... **Date** ....

FINDING ANSWERS

Where I found my answer			
Answer			
Question			
	1	2	3

Name .... **Date** ....

REPORT WRITING

My Report

Title _____

I found out about _____

_____

_____

_____

_____

_____

I learned that _____

_____

_____

_____

_____

_____

WRITING FRAMES MADE EASY • Questions and answers • page 4 of 4

© pfp 2001 ISBN 1 874050 79 1 pfp, 61 Gray's Inn Road, London WC1X 8TH May be photocopied for use within the purchasing institution only. **pfp**

Note making and report writing

Report

NLS Y2 T3 non-fiction 15, 16, 19, 20

QCA Science Unit 2b Plants and animals in the local environment. Exploring local areas gives the children many important opportunities to write reports on the types of plants and animals they discover there.

Lesson notes

For this lesson use the Heinemann Discovery World Series. If you don't have this excellent resource then use a non-fiction book from your library at an appropriate level for the children and on a subject you are studying as part of the science curriculum.

Divide your subject into smaller units and give each group a different area to research. For example, if you are studying ponds, one group can have plants to research and another group, amphibians.

During shared reading familiarise the children with the differences between fiction and non-fiction – show them how to read clues in the title, cover and the layout of the text for example. The objective for this part of the lesson is to introduce the contents and index pages. Show these to the children and model using these pages to find specific pieces of information on your subject. Ask the children to come up with questions for you.

During group or independent work allow the children to generate questions and find answers from the reference books you have given them.

Use Frame 1 Note Making and ask the children to record the chapter headings and page numbers they used from the contents page and the words and page numbers from the index page. Then ask them to record this information in simple sentences.

During shared writing ask the children to share the information they have collected. Put the title, say 'amphibians', on a blank sheet and then add a sub-heading – 'frogs' for example. Ask the group studying amphibians to share their information and begin to sort it into boxes with titles such as 'appearance', 'food', 'life cycle' and 'enemies'.

Use the remaining two writing frames as follows.

- Frame 2 Organising Information. This frame allows children to take the information they have gathered and begin to group it. They can refer back to the books they are using to gather additional information.

- Frame 3 My Report. This frame gives the layout of the final report. Children will be surprised to find how much they are able to write when given a structure like this.

During the plenary collect all the work and hold it together in a bundle. Ask the children what they would need to do to the collection of work to turn it into a class book. You are aiming to draw out that they would need to add a contents and index page, a front and back cover and bind it.

Teaching points

At this early stage in their development as report writers it is important for children to understand that they are not simply copying information from a text. The use of writing frames supports this and demonstrates the way they are carefully selecting pieces of information that suit their task and rearranging these into a meaningful piece of new text. This helps establish a good foundation for future development in this genre.

Read a non-fiction book as a class reader from time to time to help children appreciate the value of these books.

Follow up work

In design and technology explore some simple bookmaking techniques such as making zigzag books. Then in art get the children to illustrate a front cover. Bookmaking helps children value their report writing and helps them understand the purpose to their research. Over time, it will also help you stock your book corner with content specific to the subjects you cover in class.

Name .... **Date** ....

NOTE MAKING

Contents page headings	Page number

Index words	Page number

I discovered

1 _____

_____

2 _____

_____

3 _____

_____

Name .... **Date** ....

ORGANISING INFORMATION

My chapter heading   _____

My page heading   _____

Sub-heading: _____

Notes: _____

_____

_____

Sub-heading: _____

Notes: _____

_____

_____

Name .... **Date** ....

MY REPORT

My title _____

Introduction

I have been finding out about _____

_____

_____

_____

Sub-heading: _____

I learned that _____

_____

_____

_____

Sub-heading: _____

Did you know that _____

_____

_____

_____ ?

WRITING FRAMES MADE EASY • **Note making and report writing** • page 4 of 4
© pfp 2001 ISBN 1 874050 79 1 pfp, 61 Gray's Inn Road, London WC1X 8TH May be photocopied for use within the purchasing institution only.

pfp

How it works

Explanation

NLS Y1 T3 non-fiction 17, 21

QCA Science Unit 1e Pushes and pulls. After making a familiar object start moving by pushing or pulling, children write a simple account explaining their investigation and how they caused the object to move.

Lesson notes

Before the lesson look, with the children, at movement in familiar objects such as swings, roundabouts, seesaws and toys that move. Ask the children to suggest words to describe the movement such as 'push', 'pull', 'up', 'down', 'roll', 'turn', 'slide', 'twist', 'fast' and 'slow'. List these words and display them in the classroom. When the children find things that need to be pushed or pulled, ask them to explain how they made each object move, using words from your class list.

During shared reading look at some explanatory texts – ideally related to your work in science. Make clear to the children that these texts explain how or why something happens. Share lots of examples and help them spot the structure of the text, that is, it starts with an introductory statement, then explains how or why something happens in a series of logical steps and ends with a final statement. Point out the use of words such as 'first', 'then', 'next' and 'because'.

During shared writing talk with the children about how they could write up their own explanations of how they moved the objects. Make up a simple writing frame for explanation – use Frame 1 My Explanation 1 as a starting point or use one of your shared reading texts. Include the features identified during shared reading.

During guided writing complete the writing frames. Model how to complete the sentences and how to use the topic word bank. Encourage children to retell their experiments and use new words from the topic bank. Use the frames to support them in using a wider range of connectives and subject-specific vocabulary. Support your less able children by providing topic word labels that the children can select and copy. Use Frames 2 and 3 to extend the children's thinking.

- Frame 1 My Explanation 1. This introduces a simple explanation layout. Children will be familiar with this if you have used it during shared writing.

- Frame 2 My Explanation 2. This requires children to consider why the toy moved.

- Frame 3 Comparing How Two Toys Move. Use this frame to introduce the idea of comparison. Encourage the children to write about one toy that needed pushing and one that needed pulling.

During the plenary ask selected children to explain how they moved their toy to a class teddy or puppet. This will reinforce the skills of explanation.

Teaching points

Make a display from the lesson. Put the toys from the lesson alongside the children's written explanations – laminate them if you want a more permanent display. Ask them to draw pictures or diagrams to accompany the explanations and add labels or captions. As an extra activity, ask the children to check the explanations against how they move the toys. When the display has been up for long enough, put the children's explanations into a class book titled 'How Toys Move'.

Involving parents

Ask children to bring in a toy from home that moves by being pushed or pulled. If it is not practical to bring the toy into class, children could take home a copy of Frame 1 My Explanation 1 to record how their toy moves. Write a brief note to parents explaining how this activity relates to the children's work in science and literacy.

Name .... **Date** ....

MY EXPLANATION 1

I want to explain how I moved a _____

_____

_____

_____

First I _____

_____

_____

_____

Then it _____

_____

_____

_____

WRITING FRAMES MADE EASY • How it works • page 2 of 4

© pfp 2001 ISBN 1 874050 79 1 pfp, 61 Gray's Inn Road, London WC1X 8TH May be photocopied for use within the purchasing institution only.

Name .... **Date** ....

MY EXPLANATION 2

I want to explain how I _____

_____

First I _____

_____

_____

_____

Then it _____

_____

_____

_____

This is because _____

_____

_____

_____

© pfp 2001 ISBN 1 874050 79 1 pfp, 61 Gray's Inn Road, London WC1X 8TH May be photocopied for use within the purchasing institution only.

Name ....   **Date** ....

COMPARING HOW TWO TOYS MOVE

I want to explain how _____

First I _____

_____

Then it _____

_____

This is because _____

_____

I want to compare this with _____

_____

First I _____

_____

Then it _____

_____

This is because _____

_____

WRITING FRAMES MADE EASY • How it works • page 4 of 4
© pfp 2001 ISBN 1 874050 79 1 pfp, 61 Gray's Inn Road, London WC1X 8TH May be photocopied for use within the purchasing institution only. pfp

Why it happened

Explanation

NLS Y2 T3 non-fiction 16, 20

QCA History Unit 5 How do we know about the Great Fire of London? Ask the children to consider the cause and effect of the Great Fire then get them to communicate their findings to others by writing an explanation text.

Lesson notes

Before using the writing frames deliver those aspects of the history unit that allow children to identify the causes of the fire, why it ended and the results of the fire. Help children match sentence beginnings to sentence endings, for example 'The fire spread because … of the direction of the wind', 'The people escaped to the churches because … these were built of stone' or 'The fire went out because … the wind stopped'. Help children to write more sentence beginnings and endings to add to this game of 'heads and tails'.

During shared reading look at a range of non-fiction texts. Demonstrate how to scan the title, contents, illustrations, headings and sub-headings to find out what a book is about. List these features and display the list.

Collect examples of the language of time used to link sentences, for example 'first', 'next', 'after', 'during' and 'finally' from non-fiction texts. Add these to the display.

During shared writing start creating a writing frame. Ask the children to suggest suitable headings and sub-headings to explain the events of the Great Fire. Examples are given in Frame 1. Record these onto A3 paper for the structure of the frame.

During a further session use enlarged copies of the 'heads and tails' sentence beginnings. Ask children to decide which sub-heading to place each one under. This will result in a simple writing frame. Model for the children how to complete these sentences.

During guided writing use the frames as follows.

- Frame 1 The Great Fire of London. This frame highlights the use of headings and sub-headings. It uses examples of sentences in the 'heads and tails' game. Support your less able children by providing them with the sentence endings to choose from.

- Frame 2 The Start of the Great Fire of London. This frame encourages children to use the language of time to start their sentences. Provide them with the class list of these words.

- Frame 3 The Cause and Effect of the Fire of London. This frame challenges your more able children by only providing the headings and sub-headings. Encourage the children to write their own explanations.

During the plenary help children reflect on their own writing. Encourage them to find sentences that explain how the fire started and ended. Ask them to locate words that show the order of events. This reinforces the key features of an explanation text.

Teaching points

Collect and display a range of pictures showing London before, during and after the Great Fire, including recent pictures. Encourage children to add captions to the pictures indicating the cause and effect of events.

Collect examples of words and expressions that are used to describe reasons and results, for example 'because', 'reason', 'result' and 'effect'. Stress that these words are used when we write an explanation of how or why something happens.

Follow up work

With your class, predict the content of other books based on the title, illustrations, contents page, headings and sub-headings. Make this a regular feature of shared reading sessions.

In art, encourage children to communicate their understanding of the Great Fire by painting or drawing pictures of the events. Display these illustrations with their written explanations.

Name .... **Date** ....

THE GREAT FIRE OF LONDON

Why the Great Fire of London started

The fire started because _____

_____

_____

What happened during the Great Fire of London

The fire spread because _____

_____

_____

Why the Great Fire of London ended

The fire went out because _____

_____

_____

WRITING FRAMES MADE EASY • Why it happened • page 2 of 4
© pfp 2001 ISBN 1 874050 79 1 pfp, 61 Gray's Inn Road, London WC1X 8TH May be photocopied for use within the purchasing institution only. **pfp**

Name .... **Date** ....

THE START OF THE GREAT FIRE OF LONDON

Why the Great Fire of London started

_____ *the fire started because* _____

_____

What happened during the Great Fire of London

_____ *the fire spread because* _____

_____

Why the Great Fire of London ended

_____ *the fire went out because* _____

_____

_____

The results of the Great Fire of London

_____ *because of the Great Fire of London* _____

_____

_____

© pfp 2001 ISBN 1 874050 79 1 pfp, 61 Gray's Inn Road, London WC1X 8TH May be photocopied for use within the purchasing institution only.

Name .... **Date** ....

THE CAUSE & EFFECT OF THE FIRE OF LONDON

Why the Great Fire of London started

_____

_____

What happened during the Great Fire of London

_____

_____

Why the Great Fire of London ended

_____

_____

_____

The results of the Great Fire of London

_____

_____

WRITING FRAMES MADE EASY • Why it happened • page 4 of 4

© pfp 2001 ISBN 1 874050 79 1 pfp, 61 Gray's Inn Road, London WC1X 8TH May be photocopied for use within the purchasing institution only. pfp

Writing simple instructions

Instruction

NLS Y2 T1 non-fiction 13, 15–18

QCA Information Technology Unit 2d Routes: controlling a floor turtle. Children learn how to control the movements of a floor turtle through the use of single and sequential instructions. The writing frames support children in recording their own instructions.

Lesson notes

Before the lesson ask children to bring in examples of instructions from home, such as those for board games and recipes.

During shared reading compare examples of simple written instructions. Identify common features, for example a statement of purpose, a list of required materials, numbered steps set out in a sequential list, diagrams or illustrations, use of imperative verbs such as 'cut' and 'turn' and use of chronological vocabulary such as 'first' and 'next'.

Before shared writing tell the children a story about searching for hidden treasure. (This and the notes below relate closely to the integrated task in the Information Technology Unit 2d.)

During shared writing model how to write simple instructions for finding the treasure. Distribute A4 copies of a simple treasure map and ask the children to suggest an instruction to follow on from those you have just modelled. Then check your combined writing against the features of instructional texts and add any missing ones, for example a list of items that the pirate might need such as a map or a shovel. Discuss why these additional features are necessary.

During group work give each group a different location on the map in which to hide their treasure. Tell them they must write a set of instructions to direct the pirate to the treasure. They must all start at the landing bay.

- Use Writing Frame 1 Finding the Treasure to remind children of the key features of written instructions.

Reproduce the landmarks from your treasure map in the hall or the playground. Use tape and label objects in the hall to mark key features. Ask groups to exchange and read out their instructions then say where they think treasure is. Ask each group is to follow the instructions and check their accuracy. They can note any errors and make corrections later.

During the plenary review the effectiveness of the groups' instructions and highlight the need to test instructions and then amend them.

Outside of the literacy hour, engage in the 'setting the scene' and 'short focused tasks' as described in the information technology unit of work. Children can now translate their instructions for the floor turtle.

- Frame 2 Turtle's Treasure, provides prompts for a common recording method, for example F = forward. Model how to use this.

Ask children to take turns to programme the turtle using the written instructions. They are to predict the route and then make amendments after testing them out. Errors will remind children of the need to provide an accurate set of instructions in sequential order.

Teaching points

Emphasise that instructions are useful because they enable you to repeat an activity without having to remember it. Instructions let you, or someone else, complete an activity without having to ask someone what to do.

Display the variety of instructions that children brought into school. Alongside these, display pictures of equipment for which you need to follow instructions, for example washing machines, microwave ovens, photocopiers and robots.

Display your treasure map together with the children's written instructions for each other and for the floor turtle.

Involving parents

Ask parents to help their child write a series of instructions for getting from home to school. Use Frame 3 Directions from My House to School.

Name ....   **Date** ....

FINDING THE TREASURE

Instructions for _____

_____

You will need _____

_____

_____

Start at the landing bay

Use these words to help you: 'turn', 'walk', 'forwards', 'left', 'right', 'go', 'steps'

1 _____

2 _____

3 _____

4 _____

5 _____

6 _____

WELL DONE! YOU HAVE FOUND THE TREASURE!

WRITING FRAMES MADE EASY • Writing simple instructions • page 2 of 4

© pfp 2001 ISBN 1 874050 79 1 pfp, 61 Gray's Inn Road, London WC1X 8TH May be photocopied for use within the purchasing institution only.

Name ....   **Date** ....

TURTLE'S TREASURE

Instructions for _____

_____

You will need _____

_____

_____

Programme your floor turtle with the following instructions

Use this key: F = forwards, B = backwards, L= left and R = right

1 _____

2 _____

3 _____

4 _____

5 _____

6 _____

**Place your floor turtle at the landing bay, facing forwards.
Start your turtle and test your instructions.
Can your turtle find the treasure?**

© pfp 2001 ISBN 1 874050 79 1 pfp, 61 Gray's Inn Road, London WC1X 8TH May be photocopied for use within the purchasing institution only.

Name .... **Date** ....

DIRECTIONS FROM MY HOUSE TO SCHOOL

Instructions for _____

_____

You will need _____

_____

_____

From my house

Use these words to help you: turn, walk, forwards, left, right, go

First _____

Then _____

Next _____

Walk _____

Then _____

Finally _____

_____

YOU WILL NOW BE AT MY SCHOOL!

WRITING FRAMES MADE EASY • Writing simple instructions • page 4 of 4
© pfp 2001 ISBN 1 874050 79 1 pfp, 61 Gray's Inn Road, London WC1X 8TH May be photocopied for use within the purchasing institution only. pfp

Rhyming Poetry

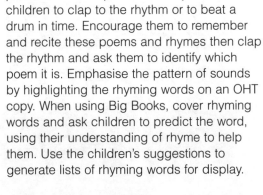

Poetry

NLS Y1 T1 fiction & poetry 6, 10

QCA Information Technology Unit 1a Assembling texts. Children use a mouse to select and drag.

Information Technology Unit 1b Using a word bank. Children use a word-processor to assemble text from a word bank.

Lesson notes

During shared reading use repetitive and predictable short poems and rhymes. Ask children to clap to the rhythm or to beat a drum in time. Encourage them to remember and recite these poems and rhymes then clap the rhythm and ask them to identify which poem it is. Emphasise the pattern of sounds by highlighting the rhyming words on an OHT copy. When using Big Books, cover rhyming words and ask children to predict the word, using their understanding of rhyme to help them. Use the children's suggestions to generate lists of rhyming words for display.

During shared writing use rhymes as models for the children's writing. Copy out a familiar rhyming poem. Ask children to suggest substitutions for rhyming words or phrases. Encourage them to suggest new verses for familiar poems, copying the pattern. Model being a writer by scribing their suggestions and developing their ideas.

During guided writing build on these shared experiences. The writing frames that follow use rhymes to encourage children's writing. Develop speaking and listening skills by asking children to listen to the rhymes and orally generate alternatives. Ask children to select their favourite rhyme to write onto their own frame or you can scribe for them.

- Frame 1 Rhyming Words. Read the whole poem and encourage children's personal responses. Distribute the frame and point out that some of the words are missing. Model how to suggest rhyming words to fill the gaps and ask for suggestions. These can be nonsense words. Children can substitute their favourites.

- Frame 2 Rhyming Phrases. This frame is based on the rhyme 'One, two, buckle my shoe'. The structure remains the same but children suggest alternative phrases. Read the original poem, model the activity, encourage suggestions and help children to record their choices on the writing frame.

- Frame 3 Rhyming Verses. The objective of this frame is to generate a new verse for a familiar poem. Model how to do this by copying the pattern and structure of the original poem. An example is provided on the frame. Work with the children to produce a third verse.

During the plenary ask children to read or recite their poems. Praise their attempts and acknowledge their skills as poets, drawing out the different rhymes and phrases used.

Teaching points

Read some of the children's new versions of well-known poems during shared reading sessions. Children love hearing and reading their own creations. Mount these poems in a class book and place it in the class reading corner.

Tape record poems for the children to listen to and let children tape record their own versions.

 ICT

Use a program such as 'My World' to match the beginning and ends of rhyming sentences. Also type in a rhyming text, leaving out the final rhyming words. Ask children to select a word from a word bank to complete each rhyme. Print and display the work.

Name .... **Date** ....

RHYMING WORDS

To market, to market,
to buy a fat pig.
Home again, home again,
jiggety jig.

To market, to market,
to buy a fat hog.
Home again, home again,
joggety jog.

To market, to market,

to buy a fat _____ .

Home again, home again,

_____ _____ .

To market, to market,

to buy a fat _____ .

Home again, home again,

 _____ _____ .

WRITING FRAMES MADE EASY • Rhyming poetry • page 2 of 4

Name .... **Date** ....

RHYMING PHRASES

One, two,
Buckle my shoe.
Three, four,
Knock at the door.
Five, six,
Pick up sticks.
Seven, eight,
Lay them straight.
Nine, ten,
A big fat hen.

One, two,

I went to the zoo

Three, four,

_____

Five, six,

_____

Seven, eight,

_____

Nine, ten,

_____

Name ....   **Date** ....

RHYMING VERSES

Humpty Dumpty sat on a wall,
Humpty Dumpty had a great fall.
All the king's horses and all the king's men,
couldn't put Humpty together again.

Humpty Dumpty stood on a chair,
Humpty Dumpty had long curly hair.
All of his shoes and all of his socks,
he kept wrapped up in a cardboard box.

My own verse

_____

_____

_____

_____

_____

_____

_____

Humorous verse

Poetry

NLS Y2 T3 fiction & poetry 6, 8, 11

QCA Information Technology Unit 2a Writing stories. Children correct and improve their work using ICT.

Information Technology Unit 2b Creating pictures. Children create pictures using a computer graphics package.

Lesson notes

During shared reading encourage children to respond to a range of humorous poetry. Ask them to select their favourites, identify the words or phrases that make them laugh and explain why they are funny. Help classify the poems by type, for example nonsense poems, tongue twisters (Dr Seuss provides some excellent examples), limericks and riddles. Encourage children to identify features such as alliteration. When reading enlarged texts, compare different poets such as Lear, Milligan, McGough, Rosen, Causley and Cope.

During shared writing select a class favourite such as 'Please Mrs Butler' by Allan Ahlberg. Substitute the teacher's name with your own and the child's name with a child in your class. Or select a poem such as 'Breakfast for One' by Judith Nicholls that plays with word order. Write a phrase such as 'warm sweet crumbly sticky pudding'. Then, with the children, keep changing the order of the words until you have exhausted all possibilities. Model reading the sentences back to check how they sound and to listen to the effect they cause. Encourage the building of nonsense words such as used in 'Jabberwocky' by Lewis Carroll. Brainstorm alternatives and note these on the board.

During group activities use the writing frames to provide models for humorous verse.

- Frames 1 and 2 Alliterative Alphabet 1 and 2. These frames support children in producing alliterative writing. Give each group one part of the alphabet and ask them to generate a list of alliterative words for each letter on their frame. In pairs, ask them to select from the suggestions to complete their own poem. Frame 1 requires children to generate alliterative nouns. Frame 2 requires children to generate alliterative nouns and adjectives. Provide dictionaries. (Note that the letters 'X' and 'Z' are missing from the alphabet here.)

- Frame 3 Humorous Verse, provides an example of a well-known rhyme together with an alternative version 'Twinkle, Twinkle Little Bat!'. Get children to work in pairs to write a further version.

During the plenary invite children to read their humorous verse aloud. Share in their enjoyment as they make their classmates laugh. Ask the class to identify what works well in the poems.

Teaching points

Extend children's experience of humorous verse and support them in writing their own through the following activities.

- Copy out a nonsense poem and cut it up into individual lines. Get the children to put it back together in their own order. Share the new versions and compare how well they work.

- Use your word bank to create nonsense poems. Distribute the words so that each child has four. Challenge them to write a poem that must include all of these words.

- Ask children to bring in favourite funny poems and hold recital sessions. Copy them into a class book to be shared during reading sessions. You will soon find that children have learned their favourites by heart and request them frequently!

- Challenge children to solve riddles.

- Have a competition – who can read the chosen tongue-twister the fastest?

SEN variation

For a variation on Frames 1 and 2, provide a range of adjectives and nouns which can be paired according to their initial sounds, eg. 'cross' and 'crab'. Write these on paper. Ask children to look at them, put them into pairs that start with the same sound and then draw a picture of each. Alternatively, write the descriptions, eg. 'cross crab', in a list on paper and each word on a card. With a partner, children can play a game of pelmanism. Place the cards face down on the table and collect pairs by turning over the cards one at a time, replacing the card if it doesn't make a pair. The player with the most pairs wins.

Name ....   **Date** ....

ALLITERATIVE ALPHABET 1

A is for angry   *alligators*

B is for bouncy   *balls*

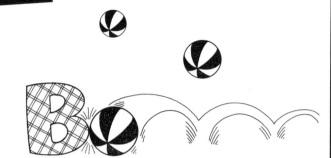

C is for clever _____

D is for dangerous _____

E is for enormous _____

F is for funny _____

G is for greedy _____

H is for happy _____

I is for intelligent _____

J is for jolly _____

K is for kind _____

L is for lovely _____

WRITING FRAMES MADE EASY • Humorous verse • page 2 of 4
© pfp 2001 ISBN 1 874050 79 1 pfp, 61 Gray's Inn Road, London WC1X 8TH May be photocopied for use within the purchasing institution only.

Name .... **Date** ....

ALLITERATIVE ALPHABET 2

M is for *mysterious monsters*

N is for *noisy noses*

O is for _____

P is for _____

Q is for _____

R is for _____

S is for _____

T is for _____

U is for _____

V is for _____

W is for _____

Y is for _____

Name .... **Date** ....

HUMOROUS VERSE

Twinkle, twinkle little star,
How I wonder what you are,
High above the world so high,
Like a diamond in the sky.
Twinkle, twinkle little star,
How I wonder what you are.

Twinkle, twinkle little bat!
How I wonder what you're at!
Up above the world you fly,
Like a tea-tray in the sky.
Twinkle, twinkle –
Twinkle, twinkle, twinkle, twinkle.

by Lewis Carroll

Twinkle, twinkle little _____

How I wonder _____

_____

Like a _____

Twinkle, twinkle _____

_____

WRITING FRAMES MADE EASY • Humorous verse • page 4 of 4
© pfp 2001 ISBN 1 874050 79 1 pfp, 61 Gray's Inn Road, London WC1X 8TH May be photocopied for use within the purchasing institution only.

Story plotting

Narrative

NLS Y1 T2 fiction & poetry 4, 14

QCA Geography Unit 1 Around our school – the local area. Children describe their route to school. This link is worth making – it is useful as a recount exercise and leads into simple map drawing skills, which can be used as a structure for plotting stories.

Lesson notes

Before the lesson ask the children to complete the homework activity at the foot of this page – using Frame 1 My Route to School. Tell the children that this map of their journey to school is a map of the story of their journey and you are going to use maps to help tell other stories. Invite several children to 'read' the story of their journey to school using their map as a prompt.

During shared reading take a well-known traditional tale. Tell the story first and then share a big book version. Explain to the children that knowing the order of events helps them tell the story without a book. Ask them to retell the story sitting in a circle taking it in turns to tell the next part.

During shared writing draw a map of the story you have chosen and use arrows to join up the events. Use sketches to illustrate the map and to help outline the tale. Use captions beneath the sketches and speech bubbles to build up a map of the story. Tell another traditional tale or use a big book. Use this story for the next part of this lesson.

During group or independent work use the writing frames as follows.

- Frame 2 Story Mapping. This frame uses arrows, captions and sketches – it shows that the sequence of the plot needs to be clear on their map. After several attempts at mapping well-known stories the children can try making up a story of their own and creating a story map for it – give them a starting point for this.

- Frame 3 Story Writing. This frame allows the children to now write their story in full. Using verbal prompts it gives them a basic plot-structuring device.

During the plenary give children the opportunity to share their own stories with the class. Focus on the sequence of events within the story.

Teaching points

Use a wealth of traditional tales during this important stage in the development of story writing skills. The transition to writing their own stories will be so much easier when children have the fertile soil of stories already written in which to grow their ideas.

Develop the sequencing of events by asking children to retell their own story in the form of a cartoon strip. The box-by-box structure of this format helps children see the sequence more clearly than text alone.

Narrative is a fictional recount and Year 1 is a good time to make it clear to children that they can tell real news and they can tell made-up news – when they are telling made-up news it is a story or narrative.

Role-play helps engage children and to develop characters and reinforce the sequence of the story in the child's mind. It is also fun – use it whenever you are writing narratives, or stories.

 Homework ideas

Send the children home with Frame 1 My Route to School. Included in the frame is a brief note to parents asking them to help their child write a description of the route they take to school and to draw a simple map. The note explains that this will be used to develop their child's story writing skills in the literacy hour.

Name .... **Date** ....

MY ROUTE TO SCHOOL

Dear Parents,

Please help your child draw a sketch map of their route to school and write a brief description of their route. This will help us to develop story writing skills in the literacy hour.

Map

Description

First _____

_____

Then _____

_____

After that _____

_____

WRITING FRAMES MADE EASY • Story plotting • page 2 of 4
© pfp 2001 ISBN 1 874050 79 1 pfp, 61 Gray's Inn Road, London WC1X 8TH May be photocopied for use within the purchasing institution only.

Name .... **Date** ....

STORY MAPPING

1

Caption

_____

_____

2

Caption

_____

_____

3

Caption

_____

_____

4

Caption

_____

_____

© pfp 2001 ISBN 1 874050 79 1 pfp, 61 Gray's Inn Road, London WC1X 8TH May be photocopied for use within the purchasing institution only.

Name .... **Date** ....

STORY WRITING

Title _____

Where does the story happen? _____

_____

_____

Who is in it? _____

_____

_____

_____

What do they do? _____

_____

_____

_____

What happens at the end? _____

_____

_____

_____

WRITING FRAMES MADE EASY • **Story plotting** • page 4 of 4
pfp

Story settings

Narrative

NLS Y2 T1 fiction & poetry 5, 13

QCA Geography Unit 6 Investigating our local area. It is helpful to develop the writing of descriptions of real settings as a starting point. Children write descriptions of places they know to give them the structure to write about places they can imagine.

Lesson notes

Note to teachers. The skills developed here take time and it may be that you will use these notes over several lessons.

During shared reading read a well-known story to the children and ask them to listen with their eyes closed. Go back to a particular point in the story where there is a definite location mentioned – such as a wood or a bridge over a stream – but where not too much detail is given. Ask the children what they see in their mind's-eye when you mention this place in the story.

During shared writing write down their responses in note form on your board. Reinforce simple sentence writing by taking one or two of the ideas and writing them up in sentence form.

During group work ask the children to talk about their mental image of the setting and prepare them to use Writing Frame 1 during individual work.

During independent work use the writing frames as follows.

- Frame 1 In My Own Words. This frame gives the children a structure in which to describe a setting. Ask the children to work in pairs to discuss how they see the setting in their mind's eye. Ask them to draw the setting and then to write a short description of it (or vice versa). Share these descriptions and take this opportunity to highlight good use of descriptive words.

During the next lesson remind the children of the work you have been doing. To illustrate the importance of the setting, discuss possible alternative story lines that the same characters could be involved in while in this setting. For example could a completely different story emerge when Red Riding Hood met the Big Bad Wolf in the woods? Let the children discuss this further in groups before using Writing Frame 2.

- Frame 2 A New Story in an Old Place. This frame gives children the layout to write a brief plan of the old and the new story and to illustrate the new story.

Discuss local places that would make a good setting for a story before using Writing Frame 3.

- Frame 3 A Place of My Own. This frame helps children develop their skills in writing about settings by describing a familiar local place in preparation for a new story. It provides children with a good structure to use their visual recall skills to describe a local setting.

During each of the plenary sessions take time to draw together the various elements you have been working on and make links with the previous and following sessions. Setting, characters and plot structure are all important elements of the story writing process and children need to have explicit links made between them.

Teaching points

Attention to description of characters and settings is the key element that differentiates narrative writing from recount.

Develop the description of setting alongside work on characters and plot structure to really give children the tools they need to write exciting and imaginative stories.

Take a story to pieces with children. Once they have heard a good story several times go through it and discuss the way the author has described settings and characters.

Follow up work

Children need time to put together the various elements given in the lessons above and they need time for additional work on characters and plots. To help and encourage this process give them the opportunity to write their own story after preliminary work. Remember that they may need an extended period to do this so try and put some time aside outside the literacy hour.

Name ....

Date ....

IN MY OWN WORDS

What I saw in my mind's eye

I saw _____

_____

I heard _____

_____

I could touch _____

_____

I could smell _____

_____

WRITING FRAMES MADE EASY • Story settings • page 2 of 4

© pfp 2001 ISBN 1 874050 79 1 pfp, 61 Gray's Inn Road, London WC1X 8TH May be photocopied for use within the purchasing institution only.

Name .... **Date** ....

A NEW STORY IN AN OLD PLACE

The old story

The new story

Draw your new idea

Name .... **Date** ....

A PLACE OF MY OWN

My place is called _____

I chose it because _____

_____

_____

A picture of my place

A description of my place

Sights: _____

_____

Sounds: _____

_____

Feelings: _____

_____

WRITING FRAMES MADE EASY • Story settings • page 4 of 4

© pfp 2001 ISBN 1 874050 79 1 pfp, 61 Gray's Inn Road, London WC1X 8TH May be photocopied for use within the purchasing institution only.

Using writing frames in Key Stage 2

Introduction

This stand-alone section for Key Stage 2 provides a range of ready-to-use photocopiable writing frames supported by teacher's notes. These sheets provide additional suggestions for meeting the needs of all children. There are examples of differentiated and cross-curricular writing frames. These curriculum links are identified in the Key Stage 2 links table on page 72.

Writing frames are a support to writing – they are the scaffolding that is in place to help the child develop the skills of writing for themselves. When used as a teaching tool,

rather than simply as photocopiable worksheets, they will contribute to the learning process and will support children in becoming independent writers. Once children are familiar with the text form and are confident, the frame can be removed, leaving the children able to write imaginatively and with creativity.

The case studies given on pages 14, 16, 18, 20 and 22 demonstrate how to use writing frames effectively in Key Stage 2 classes. Additional guidance is given on pages 70–71.

Summary of teaching guidance provided on pages 5–10

Writing frames direct children's attention to features of different texts. These include purpose and audience, structure and layout, grammar, punctuation and vocabulary. They also challenge children to widen their writing experiences. They can support writing within a new genre, especially for children who are experiencing difficulty in developing or sustaining an aspect of writing. Careful assessment of children's independent writing will indicate whether a child would benefit from using a writing frame.

To get the most out of writing frames, teachers need to share good quality texts with their children and use these as a model for children's writing. This writing needs to have a real purpose that children understand. Children also need to write for real audiences.

The teacher's role is to explicitly teach the features of different texts and then model the writing process. Children also need to be given adequate time to practice and reinforce their writing skills, both within the literacy hour and in other curriculum areas. The literacy hour should be seen as a workshop in which children acquire literacy skills that can then be applied across the curriculum.

Teachers can support the use of writing frames by encouraging and valuing children's attempts. A stimulating, print-rich environment should be provided. This would contain many examples of different text types and resources to support the writing process. An enlarged copy of the writing frame can also be displayed to support children's independent writing.

DIY writing frames

During the literacy hour, writing frames can be generated on paper or on the computer. They can be created and completed by the teacher, jointly between the teacher and children and collaboratively by children and their peers.

Almost anything written has the potential to become your next writing frame. Giving children the chance to design their own frames puts them on the path to independence. In designing for themselves they are evaluating the text structures, deciding what works and what doesn't and modelling their own design on an already successful format.

Writing frames are easy to make yourself (see pp7–8 for more detail). Take any form of written material and simply draw boxes on a blank sheet of paper to represent the different text structures within it. If you do this first, on your board in front of the whole class, soon all your children will be doing it. Then they'll know what to do when presented with a blank piece of paper – draw a frame and complete it for themselves.

Removing the scaffolding

Taking away the supportive structures of printed writing frames is not something that should be left until the end of Year 6. When you feel that children are confident in a particular aspect of a genre, then try a blank piece of paper and see how they get on. Are they still able to layout a well structured piece

of writing? This moment comes for different children at different times depending on their ability and experience in the format. Many children grasp the basic structure of letter writing in Year 3 and no longer need a writing frame for letters to a friend, but they may need one when it comes to writing a letter for an unfamiliar purpose such as a thank you letter.

It is important that you keep copies of children's completed writing frames and the ensuing pieces of finished work in an assessment folder. This will allow you to plot the development of individual children as they move towards independence in their writing.

Using writing frames in Year 3

This is a crucial year in which the foundation skills developed during Key Stage 1 are embedded and become part of the tool kit of skills that the child will use throughout the rest of their formal education and beyond.

New forms of writing are introduced in Year 3 and children should grow with these new opportunities. Non-fiction genres such as instruction, explanation and report move beyond the basic elements to allow children to begin to use these formats in real situations. Recount moves on to become a whole range of choices for children who want to share their news. Increasingly there are opportunities to link with other areas of the curriculum. Narrative and poetry broaden their

horizons. Look at a variety of different types before asking children to model their own work on these.

Any new form of text should always be experienced first during shared reading. Shared writing allows you to use this model to show children how to lay out their work when writing in this style. Year 3 is the time to get children making their own frames. They can do this in shared writing with you as a guide. During Year 3 some children will begin to realise that they can adapt certain styles of writing to other purposes. Encourage this and discuss it whenever the occasion arises. This is something that becomes increasingly important as children move through Key Stage 2.

Using writing frames in Year 4

There is a noticeable change in the content of the Framework for teaching as Year 4 is reached. Writing becomes more concerned with the realities of the world. Children are more often asked to consider the world beyond their home, family and school and to explore and comment critically on it.

Persuasion and discussion make their first appearance and children are asked to form a point of view. Year 4 is the time when the newspaper style of writing is really developed and moves from being straightforward recount to a more persuasive style. Children are ready for this – they want to know more about the world, their opinions are forming and it is important that they are given the opportunity to constructively express these opinions.

Writing frames give children the framework to do this in a secure and purposeful way. They begin to see that the word 'argument' can have quite a positive meaning.

Children's writing of narrative and poetry continue to absorb new influences from the different styles they are exposed to. Play scripts are introduced and help children to see that there are many variations on the basic narrative genre.

Help children to gain maximum benefit from all this by using more of your shared reading and writing time to discuss in depth the features of the genres you are working with. Writing frames can be redrawn and adapted to allow children to experience more of a feeling of control over their writing. They are developing more of an individual identity and their writing can mirror this.

WRITING FRAMES MADE EASY • Using writing frames in Key Stage 2 • page 2 of 4

© pfp 2000 ISBN 1 874050 79 1 pfp, 61 Gray's Inn Road, London WC1X 8TH May be photocopied for use within the purchasing institution only. pfp

Using writing frames in Year 5

The beginning of Year 5 is a good time to take stock. In the Framework for teaching you have the opportunity to work with five of our seven genres during the first term – narrative, poetry, recount, instruction and report. Use this time to assess the children's writing skills thoroughly. Set them extended writing tasks in each of the genres, with and without writing frames. Look at the results and compare them against the National Curriculum attainment targets for writing. This will help you with your national test results predictions and, more importantly, will help you to determine the needs of every individual child and the objectives they need to develop over the last two years of their primary education.

In Year 5 children need to be given more extended tasks that allow them to use a variety of techniques to produce a presentation either in a group or individually. Group work gives opportunities for speaking and listening skills

to be refined, for texts to be critically evaluated and new models of writing to be developed.

Writing with a purpose is important throughout the primary years but it is especially important in Year 5 when children, particularly boys, can become disillusioned with the process of writing. Keep your boys on board with a greater emphasis on non-fiction genres. Link writing to science and design and technology whenever possible. Boys who can see a real purpose to writing in these curriculum areas can develop their instruction and explanation writing to a high level of competence.

Hold regular writing frame workshops where the class collaborates to design new frames. They can learn a lot about text structure by coming up with frames to be used by younger children. You can start your own school file of writing frames and give everybody the benefit of this advanced work by Year 5.

Using writing frames in Year 6

In Year 6 the use of writing frames has the following three particular benefits.

1 Their continued use will help to build on work in the previous years.

2 They can help children cope with the demands of an end of key stage writing test by giving them a known framework to adopt.

3 They can help children to develop their own systems in preparation for the move to secondary school when they are going to have to cope with writing more independently.

Keep referring to the Framework for teaching and using writing frames as teachers in earlier years have done as a way of scaffolding learning. Gradually remove these supports as children become more independent. Work with

children to develop their own frames for the genres you work with.

As end of key stage tests loom, look at past writing papers and discuss each title with the children. Which genre are they dealing with and which writing frame would they use to tackle it? Practise planning out a frame and using it to plan a piece of writing in the allotted 15 minutes. Encourage children to see a mental writing frame when they close their eyes. This is their own map or guidance system which helps them find their way around different text types. Tell them this.

As the transfer process gets under way talk to the head of English at the secondary school or schools that the children transfer to about the use of writing frames so that they can continue your good work.

And finally...

Writing frames have a great deal to offer the children of Key Stage 2. Working with the frames and lesson notes on offer here will set you firmly on the path to becoming a fan of these simple but effective tools. The next step is to go it alone. You will notice that not every objective in the Framework for teaching is covered here. Find one that isn't and be brave, give it a

go, design your own writing frames and see how they work.

The ability to write effectively is a powerful tool and one that every child should have. Writing frames are not a cure-all but fthey are an effective and worthwhile tool to use in our efforts to raise standards of writing among our children.

Key Stage 2 links table

Genre	Title	NLS Objective	QCA link	Page
Recount	**Letters, journals and reports**	Year 3 Term 3 non-fiction 16, 22	Geography Unit 9 History Units 6a, 6B and 6c	73
Recount	**Newspapers**	Year 4 Term 1 non-fiction 20, 24	History Unit 7 History Unit 19	77
Recount	**Biography and autobiography**	Year 6 Term 1 non-fiction 11, 14	Science Units 6b and 6e	81
Report	**Non-chronological reports**	Year 3 Term 1 non-fiction 20, 21, 22	Science Unit 3b	85
Report	**Developing report writing**	Year 5 Term 2 non-fiction 17, 22	Design and Technology Units 5a, 5b, 5c and 5d	89
Report	**Advanced report writing**	Year 6 Term 1 non-fiction 12, 18	Art and Design Unit 6b RE Unit 6f, ICT Unit 6a	93
Explanation	**Writing explanations**	Year 4 Term 2 non-fiction 20, 25	Science Unit 4d	97
Explanation	**Planning and refining explanations**	Year 5 Term 2 non-fiction 15, 22, 24	Science Unit 5d	101
Instruction	**The organisation of instructions**	Year 4 Term 1 non-fiction 22, 25, 26	Information Technology Unit 4e	105
Instruction	**Testing instructions**	Year 5 Term 1 non-fiction 22, 25	Design and Technology Units 5b and 5d	109
Persuasion & discussion	**Points of view**	Year 4 Term 3 non-fiction 17, 21	Geography Units 8 and 21	113
Persuasion & discussion	**Presenting a case**	Year 5 Term 3 non-fiction 14, 19	n/a	117
Persuasion & discussion	**Controversial issues**	Year 6 Term 2 non-fiction 16, 19	n/a	121
Poetry	**Onomatopoeia**	Year 3 Term 3 fiction and poetry 7, 15	Geography Units 7 and 16	125
Poetry	**Sequence of poems**	Year 6 Term 3 fiction and poetry 2, 3, 4, 13	Geography Unit 14	129
Narrative	**Story sequels**	Year 3 Term 2 fiction and poetry 1, 2, 3, 10	Information Technology Unit 3e	133
Narrative	**Descriptive settings**	Year 4 Term 2 fiction and poetry 3, 10, 13	History Unit 8	137
Narrative	**Play scripts**	Year 6 Term 1 fiction and poetry 1, 9	History Unit 11	141

Letters, journals and reports

Recount

NLS Y3 T3 non-fiction 16, 22

QCA Geography Unit 9 Village settlers links with History Units 6a, 6b and 6c which are concerned with the invaders and settlers – Roman, Saxon and Viking. A combined study involves children and encourages them to recount events in a variety of ways.

Lesson notes

Before using the frames provide opportunities for recount. Start with sports events, visits from local services and trips to the theatre or to the local library. Any work on recount starts with this type of stimulus. The literacy skills are then developed during the literacy hour.

During whole-class work develop speaking and listening skills by discussing the event. Explore how the children felt about the event or visit. What did they enjoy most? What details did only they spot? Talk through the events as they happened and highlight this sequence to the children.

During shared reading explain to the class that recounts can be written in a variety of forms such as a letter to a friend, a sports report for a newspaper or a diary entry. Share examples with the class. Sports reports are easily found but you may have to write your own letters and journal entries.

During shared writing select two forms of recount that are most appropriate to your event and model writing these for the children. Show the layout of a letter and indicate where the address goes, to whom the letter is addressed, how the text is laid out and how to sign off. For a diary entry discuss the type of words someone might choose and how these

would differ from those chosen if they were writing a letter to a friend. For a sports report show how facts and opinion can be written into the same piece by using separate paragraphs.

During independent work ask the children to plan out the sequence of events in their recount by writing short, simple sentences with arrows joining them. Then ask them to work on two of the following writing frames.

- Frame 1 Telling Your Journal. This frame gives the basic format of a journal and encourages children to express their feelings about the event.

- Frame 2 Telling a Friend. This frame gives the basic format of a letter and allows children to write in more detail about what happened. Now their absent friend can appreciate it as well.

- Frame 3 Telling the World. This frame allows children to write a factual report of events while encouraging them to express an opinion.

During the plenary ask several children to read out both their recounts and discuss with the class the different approaches that each format requires.

Teaching points

Focus on the key text and language features of a recount by emphasising the role of words such as 'first', 'next', 'then, 'after' and 'when'. Draw up a class list of these key words and display them prominently.

Discuss children's news on a regular basis – this is good practice and should not be seen as the sole preserve of Key Stage 1. Children need to share and discuss their news and rely on the feedback of others to guide their future actions.

Display sports reports on a special notice board and update them weekly to reflect the triumphs and defeats of your school teams. Make it clear that a sports 'report' is actually a recount.

📖 Homework ideas

Ask children to keep a journal over a half-term period. Get them to record three or four events that they have enjoyed with their family and friends during this time. When they return these recounts to school ask them to select one to rewrite in a different form.

Name .... **Date** ....

TELLING YOUR JOURNAL

Dear Diary,

Today at school we _____

_____

_____

First _____

_____

_____

After that _____

_____

_____

I felt _____

_____

_____

It was really _____

_____

_____

Name .... **Date** ....

TELLING A FRIEND

B. Mychum
26 Tree Lane
End-of-the-Garden
NE2 5XU

Your address

Date _____

Dear _____ ,

I'm writing to tell you about _____

_____

First _____

_____

_____

After that _____

_____

_____

You would have enjoyed it because _____

_____

Yours truly,

_____

Name .... **Date** ....

TELLING THE WORLD

Gazette

Headline

_____

Introduction to the event

_____

_____

_____

What happened

First _____

_____

Next _____

_____

Then _____

_____

My opinion is

_____

_____

_____

_____

WRITING FRAMES MADE EASY • Letters, journals and reports • page 4 of 4

© pfp 2001 ISBN 1 874050 79 1 pfp, 61 Gray's Inn Road, London WC1X 8TH May be photocopied for use within the purchasing institution only.

Newspapers

Recount

NLS Y4 T1 non-fiction 20, 24

QCA History Unit 7 Why did Henry VIII marry six times? This is perfect fodder for a newspaper report.

History Unit 19 What were the effects of Tudor exploration? This era provides ideal material for exaggerated headlines.

Lesson notes

Before using the frames stimulate the children's interest. An excellent way to do this is by linking newspaper reporting to a history topic. It can be equally well applied to a school event – such as a drama production – or the events in a story you are reading.

During shared reading pin the front page of a newspaper onto your board. During discussion with the children, use a marker pen to highlight features such as headlines, sub-headings, bold paragraphs, quotes, statistics, photographs and diagrams. Write the names of these features beside the sheet and draw arrows to indicate where they are.

Cut up a section of a newspaper and rearrange the contents into groups. Stick all the statistics on one piece of paper, all the headlines on another and so on. This helps the children to learn to recognise the categories they will be using.

During shared writing experiment with the short, clipped sentences of a journalistic style to recall the events you have chosen as your subject. Write the opening paragraph to your report together and indicate how important this part is to capture readers' attention.

During guided writing use the writing frames to develop the planning and writing of newspaper reports. Work with each of your groups to ensure the children understand the structures they are using.

- Frame 1 Planning a Newspaper Report. This frame takes the categories you have just identified with the children and helps the children arrange the information on the chosen subject.

- Frame 2 Writing a Factual Report. This gives the basic layout of a newspaper report with the emphasis on the factual reporting of a sequence of events.

- Frame 3 Writing a Biased Report. This gives the basic layout of a newspaper report with an accurate account of the sequence of events, but with the emphasis on opinion.

During the plenary have a headline making session. Take the subject you are studying and see who can come up with the most exaggerated or witty headline. Write these on large strips of paper and display.

Teaching points

Develop publishing and journalistic skills by undertaking the publication of a half-term school newspaper. Send reporters off to cover the many and varied events in the life of your school.

Role-play historical events that you are using as the basis of your newspaper reports. This helps children experience more directly the events and characters involved. For an even more direct experience combine this with a visit to a historical site.

Interview an editor or a journalist on your local newspaper to give children the opportunity to learn first hand about the publishing business.

 ICT

Make your own newspaper reports look more professional by using a simple desktop publishing package. This allows you to lay out the work in columns, experiment with different fonts and different-sized fonts and produce headlines and sub-headings. Print out the work and get the children to cut out the different features and experiment by sticking them onto their finished reports.

Name ....

Date ....

PLANNING A NEWSPAPER REPORT

Briefly describe the event

_____

_____

_____

_____

_____

A possible headline _____

Sub-headings
for paragraphs   _____

_____

_____

Quotes

_____

_____

_____

Statistics

_____

_____

WRITING FRAMES MADE EASY • Newspapers • page 2 of 4

© pfp 2001 ISBN 1 874050 79 1 pfp, 61 Gray's Inn Road, London WC1X 8TH May be photocopied for use within the purchasing institution only. **pfp**

Name .... **Date** ....

WRITING A FACTUAL REPORT

Gray's Gazette

Headline (big and bold)

Introduce the event

_____

_____

_____

_____

First _____

_____

_____

_____

Next _____

_____

_____

_____

After that _____

_____

_____

Give some facts (use bullet points)

• _____

• _____

• _____

• _____

• _____

Illustration or diagram

Finally

_____

_____

_____

Name ....

Date ....

WRITING A BIASED REPORT

Gray's Gazette

Headline (big and bold)

Briefly describe the event

_____

_____

_____

_____

_____

_____

_____

_____

I thought that _____

_____

_____

_____

_____

_____

Illustration

I didn't like _____

_____

_____

_____

My opinion is that _____

_____

_____

_____

_____

Biography and autobiography

Recount

NLS Y6 T1 non-fiction 11, 14

QCA Develop children's skills in biography by profiling pioneering scientists.

Science Unit 6b Micro-organisms. Look at the life and work of Louis Pasteur.

Science Unit 6e Forces in action. Produce a biography of Sir Isaac Newton.

Lesson notes

Before using the lesson notes and writing frames you will need to have covered the concepts and objectives linked to the famous scientist you have chosen to write about. This work will take place during science lessons.

The children will also need to have developed their research skills in order to build up a collection of facts about the person they are studying. This can come from the guidance and writing frames produced in Non-chronological reports on page 85.

During whole-class work explain the difference between biography and autobiography – and that they are both forms of recount.

Choose a child who knows quite a lot about your historical scientist and put them in the 'hot seat' – quite simply a seat at the front of the class. Ask the rest of the class to ask the person in the 'hot seat' questions to increase their own knowledge about this character. The child selected will be in role and will need to be able to elaborate on the answers they give. If you have no one who can fulfil this role then you can do it yourself.

During group work use the first writing frame.

- Frame 1 Biographical Notes. Ask the children to continue to share the knowledge they have gained by talking about the 'hot seating'. Ask them to make notes on this frame, beginning to work towards a chronological retelling of the person's life.

During individual work use the other two frames.

- Frame 2 A Biography of a Famous Scientist. This frame allows children to take their notes and put them into a structured account of the person's life. Point out that it is the sequencing of events that makes this a recount.

- Frame 3 My Autobiography. Finishing with an autobiography helps the children to see the difference between the two forms.

During the plenary ask the children to read parts of their autobiography that they feel comfortable sharing and, in the process, they may learn more about their classmates.

Teaching points

Develop speaking and listening skills by extending the 'hot seat' part of the lesson to give more children a chance to be interviewed.

Read autobiographies of famous people to your class as class readers. Encourage children to read some for themselves as a way of finding role models for their own lives.

Produce a class assembly on the theme of biography. This is a way of sharing with the whole school the lives of influential people who have helped humanity.

INSET

Writing Frames Made Easy gives you guidance and frames covering the development of recount skills from Years 1 to 6. They progress from sharing news to writing biographies. Share this with your colleagues and refer to the Framework for teaching to ensure your school is giving full coverage. Discuss the various ways in which you each teach recount skills and glean new ideas from each other.

Name .... **Date** ....

BIOGRAPHICAL NOTES

Name of the person _____

Date of birth _____

Place of birth _____

Notes on their early life

_____

_____

_____

_____

_____

Important dates   Major discoveries

_____   _____

_____   _____

_____   _____

_____   _____

How they helped the world

_____

_____

_____

_____

WRITING FRAMES MADE EASY • Biography and autobiography • page 2 of 4

© pfp 2001 ISBN 1 874050 79 1 pfp, 61 Gray's Inn Road, London WC1X 8TH May be photocopied for use within the purchasing institution only.

Name .... **Date** ....

A BIOGRAPHY OF A FAMOUS SCIENTIST

Title _____

I have decided to write about _____

_____

because _____

(name) _____ was born in _____ on _____

Early life

_____

_____

_____

_____

Discoveries

_____

_____

_____

_____

_____

Effect on the world

_____

_____

_____

_____

Name ....   **Date** ....

MY AUTOBIOGRAPHY

I was born in _____ on _____

When I was a baby I _____

_____

_____

My earliest memory is _____

_____

_____

_____

The day I enjoyed most was _____

_____

_____

_____

_____

The day I enjoyed least was _____

_____

_____

_____

_____

My life so far could be described as _____

_____

_____

Non-chronological reports

Report

NLS Y3 T1 non-fiction 20, 21, 22

QCA Science Unit 3b Helping plants grow well asks 'What do plants need to grow?' and leads children into research on the needs of plants. This is ideal preparation work for report writing.

Lesson notes

Non-chronological reports provide an ideal opportunity to link your literacy teaching to another subject, helping to embed the learning in both areas.

Before using the lesson notes and writing frames prepare the children with introductory work on the scientific concepts you are studying.

During shared reading use a photocopy of an extract from a non-fiction book which gives plenty of information about your subject. You will need one extract between two children and a selection of coloured pencils. Read through the extract together and ask the children to identify key scientific words and note these on your board. Agree on a colour to highlight these words and ask the children to underline them on their text. Next look at short sentences or phrases that detail the words you have chosen and highlight these in a different colour. Now look for statistics of any kind and highlight these numbers. This process helps to categorise information.

During shared writing transfer the highlighted features to a grid. Use the layout from Writing Frame 1 Gathering Information and ask the children to give you sentences that use the information gathered – write these up as well. With the children write a short introductory paragraph to the subject using some of these sentences and referring to the text structure of reports given on page 13.

During independent or group work give the children another area to research and let them use the techniques detailed above.

Use the writing frames as follows.

- Frame 1 Gathering Information. The layout of this frame allows children to arrange their information on a grid for ease of access. Ask them to use this frame after having highlighted different types of information on a photocopy of a page from a non-fiction book. Once they complete it, ask them to write their own sentences on another piece of paper in preparation for the final report.

- Frame 2 Writing a Report 1. This is a simple layout for your less able children and is suitable for use during guided writing. It uses the basic text structure of reports given on page 13.

- Frame 3 Writing a Report 2. This is for the majority of the class and produces a slightly more detailed report with a greater emphasis on the use of technical language.

During the plenary review the different research techniques the children have used. Discuss other areas of the curriculum – apart from science – in which they could use these techniques.

Teaching points

Focus on the links between literacy and other curriculum subjects. Ask children to read their reports to the class at the end of experimental work. For example, after experiments on transpiration and photosynthesis in flowering plants read some reports on different flowering plants.

A further lesson involves explanation writing (see page 15) about the feeding systems involved. This helps children compare different writing genres and see why we use certain styles for certain information.

 Homework ideas

Ask children to use these techniques to write a report on something of interest to them. Allow them to take home non-fiction books from your school library – remind them to copy out the information they require rather than draw lines under it!

When they return their reports to school make them the subject of a plenary session or put up a display of reports for other children to share.

Name .... **Date** ....

GATHERING INFORMATION

Key words	Phrases	Numbers

The main points

- _____
- _____
- _____
- _____
- _____
- _____
- _____
- _____

WRITING FRAMES MADE EASY • **Non-chronological reports** • page 2 of 4

© pfp 2001 ISBN 1 874050 79 1 pfp, 61 Gray's Inn Road, London WC1X 8TH May be photocopied for use within the purchasing institution only. pfp

Name .... **Date** ....

WRITING A REPORT 1

My report on _____

Opening

_____

_____

_____

_____

Description

What it looks like: _____

_____

_____

Where it lives: _____

_____

How it feeds: _____

_____

_____

Picture of

Name .... **Date** ....

WRITING A REPORT 2

My report on _____

Opening: _____

_____

_____

Description (use a key word in each sentence)

Appearance: _____

_____

Habitat: _____

_____

_____

Feeding: _____

_____

Reproduction: _____

_____

_____

Labelled diagram

WRITING FRAMES MADE EASY • Non-chronological reports • page 4 of 4
© pfp 2001 ISBN 1 874050 79 1 pfp, 61 Gray's Inn Road, London WC1X 8TH May be photocopied for use within the purchasing institution only.

Developing report writing

Report

NLS Y5 T2 non-fiction 17, 22

QCA Design and Technology Units 5a Musical instruments, 5b Bread, 5c Moving toys and 5d Biscuits. Combine Biscuits with work in an historical period you are studying to produce written reports during the literacy hour.

Lesson notes

Before using the lesson notes and writing frames complete the design and technology work shown in the link above (or similar work) and make the objects. This can then be extended into literacy giving children the opportunity to develop their referencing skills to find out how these objects were made and used in the past.

During shared reading pay a visit to the school library or present the class with a selection of historical reference books. Look at the features on the covers of the books, such as series and book title, author's name, publisher and ISBN number. Go into the book and model using the contents and index pages to find information. Ask the children questions and see who can give you a page reference for the answer.

During shared writing remind the children of techniques they already have to find information from texts. These include looking at chapter headings, sub-headings and boxed information within pages – and looking for key words and marking these on photocopies of texts. Posing and answering their own questions and transferring information to grids in note form are two other techniques developed earlier in their school life. Tell the children they are now going to use all these techniques to write a report to accompany their design project.

In independent work use the writing frames as a progression to develop planning, writing and refining reports as follows.

- Frame 1 Planning a Report. The format of this frame prompts children to use all the different techniques they have learned to gather information for their report. This will stop them relying too heavily on one technique only.

- Frame 2 Composing a Report. This frame gives a basic report layout and – once completed – children can write notes alongside it to say how they want to develop their report for the final presentation. Discuss with children the improvements they wish to make before moving on to the next frame.

- Frame 3 Refining a Report. This frame gives the layout in which children write their final report. At this level they need to be using more complex sentences so remember to prompt them to do this.

During the plenary talk to the children about the concept of a 'response partner' – someone who gives feedback on their writing. Feedback needs to be mainly positive with one or two pointers to improvements. Give the children time to do this in pairs and thus help each other to develop their report writing.

Teaching points

A further lesson involves the children in rewriting their reports for a younger audience. They could then take their design and make project and their report to a younger class and share what they have produced. This is good discipline in writing for different audiences.

Produce a class book in the form of a non-fiction reference containing all the information on the subject you have been studying and display this with your design and make projects. At the end of this project put it in the school library so everyone can benefit.

 Homework ideas

Children need to see a purpose to their writing. Invite a parent into the class to discuss with them how research and report writing skills help them in their work – this will make these lessons more meaningful to the children. It is important to discuss with the parent beforehand the approach you are using so they can tailor their comments accordingly.

Name .... **Date** ....

PLANNING A REPORT

Notes from contents and index pages	Key words and their meanings

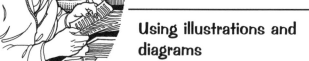

Posing and answering questions	Using illustrations and diagrams

Name .... **Date** ....

COMPOSING A REPORT

Title

Opening

Description

1 _____

_____

_____

_____

2 _____

_____

_____

_____

3 _____

_____

_____

Improving my report

_____

_____

_____

_____

_____

_____

_____

_____

_____

_____

_____

_____

_____

_____

_____

Draw arrows from your report to your ideas for improvement

Name ....   **Date** ....

REFINING A REPORT

Title ....

Opening (make sure you use detailed scientific words and explain them)

_____

_____

_____

Description (make it clear what each paragraph is about)

Sub-heading: ....

_____

_____

_____

_____

Sub-heading: ....

_____

_____

_____

_____

Sub-heading: ....

_____

_____

_____

WRITING FRAMES MADE EASY • Developing report writing • page 4 of 4

© pfp 2001 ISBN 1 874050 79 1 pfp, 61 Gray's Inn Road, London WC1X 8TH May be photocopied for use within the purchasing institution only. pfp

WRITING FRAMES *made easy*

Advanced report writing

Report

NLS Y6 T1 non-fiction 12, 18

QCA Art and Design Unit 6b
What a performance
provides a starting point.

RE Unit 6f How do
people express their faith
through the arts?

ICT Unit 6a Multimedia
presentations.

Lesson notes

Before using the lesson notes and writing frames work in Art and RE so the children have a good grounding in the subject of costume and headwear. Undertake research to gather information on the subject using all the techniques given in preceding sections of this publication (you may wish to refer back to the case study on page 14). This work allows them to take their research to final publication standard as a group multimedia presentation.

During shared reading look at printouts of pages from CD-Roms or the Internet and evaluate them together. What features work well? Does the use of coloured text, for example help capture the reader's interest and make them want to read on? What features don't work well? Are the photographs too small or the use of language unimaginative? Make notes on your board and begin to select elements the children want to have in their own presentations.

Use Writing Frame 1 Evaluating Reports at this point to extend this initial class work, or include it during the rest of the paired work session. Let the children work in pairs to write an evaluation of a printout giving information on costumes. Come back together as a class and discuss. Add more points to your list of features.

During shared writing take a report that a child has already written on costume and map out on your board how they think it will look as a presentation on screen. Where will they put titles, blocks for the text, buttons linking to other subjects?

During paired work the children can complete the remaining two writing frames.

• Frame 2 A Multimedia Presentation. This frame is designed for children to take a report they have already written using a traditional structure and rearrange the information to produce a version that can be transferred to the computer.

• Frame 3 Joined Up Thinking. This frame makes the children think about how their report links up with other reports to produce a complete reference guide. It helps them do this by using a planning sheet, which will help them produce links when they come to write their reports on the computer.

During the plenary produce a whole-class flow chart to show how everyone's reports will link up to create the finished presentation.

Outside the literacy hour children will need the time to turn their report into a multimedia presentation on screen and to publish it on the Internet.

Teaching points

Display the processes involved in producing your multimedia presentation with examples of children's evaluations, notes, plans and drafts as well as printouts of their finished pieces.

Publish your own online reference guide to costume and headwear on the Internet. Many schools are now doing this kind of work and there is a wealth of good quality factual material written by children for children. Your class can add to this.

 ICT

Practice teaching computer skills to the whole class in one session then allow the children the freedom to explore the software in pairs. They actually learn more in this way than if you try to teach them in small groups or use 'class experts' to teach other children.

Name .... **Date** ....

EVALUATING REPORTS

Name of the website _____

Website address _____

Brief description of content _____

_____

_____

What works well	What doesn't work well

Ideas I want to use

- _____
- _____
- _____
- _____
- _____
- _____

WRITING FRAMES MADE EASY • Advanced report writing • page 2 of 4
© pfp 2001 ISBN 1 874050 79 1 pfp, 61 Gray's Inn Road, London WC1X 8TH May be photocopied for use within the purchasing institution only.

Name ....

Date ....

A MULTIMEDIA PRESENTATION

Design your multimedia page here. Remember to include:

☐ A title   ☐ Blocks of text

☐ Buttons linking to sounds and images   ☐ Photographs

☐ Buttons linking to other pages   ☐ Graphics

Tick the boxes when you have included these items.

Use ideas from your written report.

Name .... **Date** ....

JOINED UP THINKING

Plot out the links you will have to other pages and give brief details of each page.

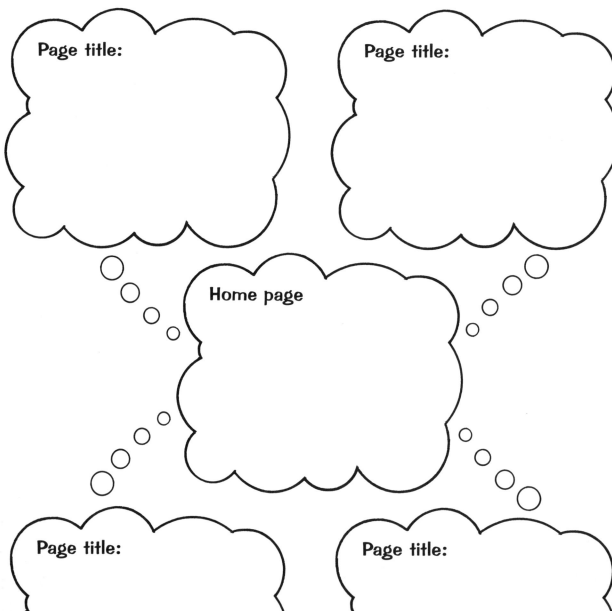

Page title:

Page title:

Home page

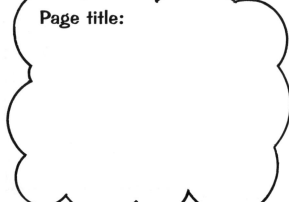

Page title:

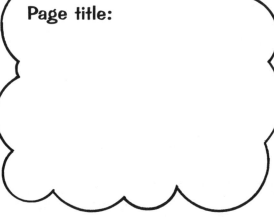

Page title:

WRITING FRAMES MADE EASY • Advanced report writing • page 4 of 4

© pfp 2001 ISBN 1 874050 79 1 pfp, 61 Gray's Inn Road, London WC1X 8TH May be photocopied for use within the purchasing institution only.

Writing explanations

Explanation

NLS Y4 T2 non-fiction 20, 25

QCA Science Unit 4d Solids, liquids and how they can be separated. Work in this unit offers opportunities for children to write explanations of processes such as melting, freezing, dissolving and filtering.

Lesson notes

Encourage oral explanations before attempting written ones. Enable children to rehearse their thoughts before committing them to paper. During the science lessons deepen children's understanding of their observations by asking them to consider questions related to 'how' and 'why'. If you are explaining a process to the class, ask them to challenge your comments and provide their own explanations.

During shared reading compare a number of explanation texts and model how to read them, for example using headings to locate information. Highlight the purpose of these texts and identify the intended audience. Through discussion, identify the features of explanation texts, including the structure, language features and use of diagrams. Record these on strips of card.

During shared writing invite children to pin these cards up in the correct order to produce a frame for writing explanation texts. Use a shared experience, for example your science investigation, to complete the frame. Model the use of subject-specific vocabulary such as 'melt', 'freeze' and 'dissolve'. Talk children through the thought processes and decisions taken by a writer, for example 'Now I need to write why the ice melted'.

During guided writing help children to gather their thoughts by brainstorming the topic. Write their contributions onto a chart for the whole group to refer to. Using your jointly constructed framework or one of the photocopiable frames, ask children to sort their contributions under each heading before writing up their explanation. Support children by providing technical vocabulary such as 'solid', 'liquid', 'melt', 'freeze' and 'solidify'.

- Frame 1 Solids and Liquids – Ice and Water. This frame gives the basic format of an explanation. Use it to help children write up their thoughts and observations as an explanation.

- Frame 2 How to Change Water to Ice and Ice to Water. This frame encourages children to move beyond simple observation and to begin to identify causes and their effects.

- Frame 3 An Explanation of Changing Ice and Water. This frame supports children in using time and causal connectives.

During the plenary ask several children to read out their explanations. Put the rest of the class into groups. Ask one group to spot examples of time connectives, another group to spot the use of connectives that relate cause to effect and a third group to check the accuracy of the explanation and how easy it is to understand. Discuss the groups' findings and use these to evaluate the effectiveness of the explanations.

Teaching points

Focus on the language features and structure of an explanation by emphasising the use of words such as 'first', 'then' and 'because'. Draw up class lists of these words and display them in the classroom.

Link explanations to topics such as writing up the findings of a science experiment. Children come to understand the world through oral and written explanations. Explaining their own learning helps children to reflect on their newly acquired knowledge.

 Homework ideas

After the children complete their written explanations, remind them of the use of diagrams and illustrations by showing examples in shared reading. Ask children to add diagrams or illustrations to their written text as a homework activity. When these are returned to school, evaluate how well they support the writing and help the reader in understanding the explanation.

Name .... **Date** ....

SOLIDS AND LIQUIDS – ICE AND WATER

This explains how to _____

_____

_____

Water is _____

_____

_____

Ice is _____

_____

_____

To turn ice into water _____

_____

_____

To turn water into ice _____

_____

Name .... **Date** ....

HOW TO CHANGE WATER TO ICE AND ICE TO WATER

An explanation of _____

_____

Ice is made from _____

_____

Water freezes when _____

_____

This is because _____

_____

Ice melts if _____

_____

This is because _____

_____

Name .... **Date** ....

AN EXPLANATION OF CHANGING ICE AND WATER

An explanation of how to _____

_____

To begin with, ice is _____

_____

When ice is taken out of _____

_____

This is because _____

_____

Water is a _____

_____

After a while, when water is _____

_____

This is because _____

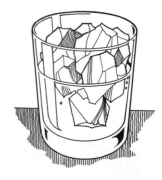

_____

WRITING FRAMES MADE EASY • Writing explanations • page 4 of 4
© pfp 2001 ISBN 1 874050 79 1 pfp, 61 Gray's Inn Road, London WC1X 8TH May be photocopied for use within the purchasing institution only. pfp

Planning & refining explanations

Explanation

NLS Y5 T2 non-fiction 15, 22, 24

QCA Science Unit 5d Changing state. Children explain a range of processes, including the water cycle. During literacy lessons they plan, draft, edit and publish their written explanations.

Lesson notes

Do these activities over a number of lessons to help children to consolidate and practise skills.

During shared reading revise the features of explanatory texts and note the features of impersonal style as described in the Framework. Jointly produce an explanation text framework.

Evaluate a range of explanation texts. After reading a section of each example ask the children to explain to a partner what they have just read. Identify which text was easiest to understand and what features it had.

During shared writing model how to plan explanatory texts using a writing frame. Frame 1 The Water Cycle Initial Brainstorm will support children in brainstorming what they know about the water cycle. Use Frame 2 The Water Cycle Planning Sheet to model categorising this information under appropriate headings.

Use this plan to jointly compose your first draft within the structure of an explanatory text, for example your jointly constructed frame or Writing Frame 3 The Water Cycle. Focus on one or more of the features of impersonal style, such as complex sentences.

Jointly edit your text and focus on impersonal style and evaluate for clarity and conciseness.

At each stage remind children of the features of effective explanatory texts.

During guided sessions use the writing frames to develop children's planning skills. Over the unit of work, support guided groups at whatever stage of the writing process they are at. Initially, guided work is likely to focus on planning. This will change to composing, editing and, finally, publication. Don't attempt to work with every group on every aspect of the writing process as there will not be time.

- Frame 1 The Water Cycle – Initial Brainstorm. This uses a visual image to help children record all they know about the water cycle. Encourage them to write words and phrases only. Provide technical vocabulary such as 'evaporation', 'condensation' and 'water cycle' to support those children who need it.

- Frame 2 The Water Cycle Planning Sheet. This gives the basic layout of an explanation text, with an emphasis on structure and headings.

- Frame 3 The Water Cycle. Use this frame after the planning process to produce a draft version of the explanation.

During the plenary ask children to evaluate their work in pairs. Focus on different aspects of the writing such as conciseness, clarity and the use of impersonal features. Finally, compare the children's explanatory texts against published resources. Identify the effective features that they have in common.

Teaching points

As children revisit text types use assessment to identify which features of each text they are confident with and which features need revisiting or introducing.

Check whether a passage is concise by highlighting key nouns and verbs and checking that key ideas have been written using the least number of words possible.

Build in time for children to add diagrams and illustrations to their work.

 ICT

Science Unit 5d is linked to the Information Technology Units 5b and 5c. These require children to obtain, collect, retrieve and present data. Use this data to support children's written explanations of the scientific processes involved in the water cycle.

Name ....   **Date** ....

THE WATER CYCLE – INITIAL BRAINSTORM

Next to each stage of the water cycle, note down any words and phrases that will help you in planning your explanation. Some words that might help you are 'evaporates', 'condenses' and 'water cycle'.

_____

_____

_____

_____

_____

_____

_____

_____

_____

_____

_____

_____

_____

WRITING FRAMES MADE EASY • Planning and refining explanations • page 2 of 4

© pfp 2001 ISBN 1 874050 79 1 pfp, 61 Gray's Inn Road, London WC1X 8TH May be photocopied for use within the purchasing institution only.

Name .... **Date** ....

THE WATER CYCLE – PLANNING SHEET

Title _____

Introductory statement identifying what is to be explained

_____

_____

Sequence of stages in the process (Explain the water cycle.
Use these words to help you: evaporates, condenses, water cycle.)

_____

_____

_____

Application (Examples of where you can see parts of this process in the home.)

_____

_____

_____

Concluding statement _____

_____

_____

© pfp 2001 ISBN 1 874050 79 1 pfp, 61 Gray's Inn Road, London WC1X 8TH May be photocopied for use within the purchasing institution only.

Name .... **Date** ....

THE WATER CYCLE

This is to explain _____

_____

As the sun shines, it _____

_____

The water _____

_____

This _____

_____

Clouds are formed from _____

_____

Next the water drops in the clouds _____

_____

Finally, it _____

_____

You can see examples of this _____

_____

To sum up _____

_____

WRITING FRAMES MADE EASY • Planning and refining explanations • page 4 of 4

© pfp 2001 ISBN 1 874050 79 1 pfp, 61 Gray's Inn Road, London WC1X 8TH May be photocopied for use within the purchasing institution only. **pfp**

Key Stage 2

The organisation of instructions

Instruction

NLS Y4 T1 non-fiction 22, 25, 26

QCA Information Technology Unit 4e Modelling effects on screen. Children enter instructions to control a screen turtle. Link this to instructional writing in the literacy hour. See also Writing simple instructions Y2 T1 on page 49.

Lesson notes

Ask the children to identify occasions when they need to refer to instructions. Discuss how instructions explain how to do something so that someone else can successfully complete the task.

Outside of the literacy hour get children to work with the screen turtle from Information Technology Unit 4e. Ask them to give oral instructions to a partner that their partner has to remember. Their partners will probably either forget the instructions or the instructions' order. Discuss the benefits of written instructions that cannot be forgotten or jumbled.

Ask children to identify, from memory, features of written instructions, for example in a recipe the list of ingredients and the series of steps. Record these and encourage children to bring examples in to be displayed, referred to and evaluated throughout the unit of work.

During shared reading read several enlarged instructions together and highlight additional features, for example an opening statement of the intended outcome, imperative verbs, linking words and phrases, present tense and diagrams and illustrations of the final outcome. Add these to the list of features.

During shared writing select a child to carry out a simple task such as sharpening pencils. Ask him or her to relate each action in their own words. For example, 'You sit close to the bin and then put the pencil into the pencil sharpener. Then you turn the pencil and keep turning it until it is sharp'. Scribe what they say, word for word, onto the flipchart. Read this back and compare it against good examples of instructions and your list of text features. Jointly edit the writing by omitting unneeded

vocabulary, substituting words, numbering the stages or adding linking phrases. For example, 'First, sit close to the bin'. 'Next, place the pencil into the pencil sharpener'. 'Then turn the pencil repeatedly until it is sharp'.

Demonstrate layout, use of diagrams, the starting point and the needs of the audience in deciding on how much detail is needed.

During group work, provide children with a purpose for their writing, for example writing instructions for the use of a screen turtle, lego model or game. The audience could be their peers, younger children or parents.

Show the children the three writing frames and ask them to select the frame that most closely meets their needs. They can use it as it stands or adapt it to suit their purposes.

• Frame 1 Instruction 1 uses numbering.

• Frame 2 Instruction 2 uses link words.

• Frame 3 Instruction 3 uses sub-headings.

Get children to test their instructions with a partner and spot errors or omissions. Ask the pair to edit the instructions and present them to the chosen audience.

During each plenary focus on a different aspect, for example the content or the use of numbering, link phrases or sub-headings. Evaluate children's own writing against the models they have read and the class list of text features.

Teaching points

Provide umbled copies of the list of features. Ask them to sequence the features to produce a writing frame and to justify their sequencing.

Photocopy a simple instructional text Jumble it and ask children to place it in order and identify the clues that helped them.

✐ INSET ideas

Writing Frames Made Easy gives you three batches of guidance and frames covering development of instructional writing from Y2 to Y5 (see also pages 49 and 109). Share these with your colleagues and refer to the Framework to ensure that your school is providing full coverage and progression of these skills. Discuss how you teach instructional writing and share ideas.

Name .... **Date** ....

INSTRUCTION 1

Opening statement: _____

_____

List of materials/equipment

_____

_____

_____

_____

_____

Diagram

Series of sequenced steps

1 _____

_____

2 _____

_____

3 _____

_____

4 _____

_____

5 _____

_____

WRITING FRAMES MADE EASY • The organisation of instructions • page 2 of 4
© pfp 2001 ISBN 1 874050 79 1 pfp, 61 Gray's Inn Road, London WC1X 8TH May be photocopied for use within the purchasing institution only. pfp

Name .... **Date** ....

INSTRUCTION 2

How to _____

You will need _____

_____

First _____

_____

Then _____

_____

Next _____

_____

After that _____

_____

Finally _____

_____

_____

Name .... **Date** ....

INSTRUCTION 3

Main heading (write your aim)

....

Sub-heading (write what you need) ....

_____

_____

_____

Sub-heading (describe how to do it) ....

_____

_____

_____

_____

Sub-heading (describe how you can
tell whether the instructions have worked) ....

_____

_____

Testing instructions

Instruction

NLS Y5 T1 non-fiction 22, 25

QCA Design and Technology Units 5b Bread and 5d Biscuits. Children explore and follow recipes then adapt them to make something of their own. They use the language of recipes, order their work and identify the required ingredients and utensils.

Lesson notes

By Year 5 children have an understanding of a range of situations where written instructions may be used and they will be familiar with the features of this text type.

Start by asking children to collect examples of recipes for biscuits and bread – current and past examples and ones from different cultures.

During shared reading explore the example recipes. Identify the vocabulary of recipes such as 'knead', 'prove', 'bake', 'flour' and 'dough'. Emphasise sequential vocabulary such as 'while', 'during', and 'then'.

Using one of the examples, model how to construct a writing frame that mirrors the features of the text. Distribute the remaining examples and ask children to use their text as a model to produce their own writing frame for recipes. Use Frame 1 Writing a Recipe 1 to support this.

During shared writing compare the writing frames that children have produced. List the similarities and identify features that are specific to certain time periods in the writing of recipes (for example the use of ounces or grammes) or to certain audiences, for example the use of illustrations in children's recipe books. Then evaluate the range of writing frames in order to jointly produce a list of criteria for effective features. Direct the children's attention to the needs of the reader

by encouraging them to question the original text: Does it meet its purpose? Is the layout easy to follow? Are the instructions clear?

During design and technology the children can go on to follow the bread or biscuit recipe before designing their own and amending the recipe. They can produce a list of their chosen ingredients and equipment and a series of steps. Ask the children to record this as a flowchart.

During independent work challenge children to transform their flowchart into a written recipe. Use Frame 2 Writing a Recipe 2 to support this activity.

During further design and technology sessions, the children can go on to test their recipes and then edit them if necessary.

Again, during independent work ask children to write their own recipe without the support of a frame in preparation for a class cookbook. This can subsequently be illustrated, perhaps with photographs of the children's products.

During the plenary review the different organisational techniques the children have used and discuss whether they meet the needs of the reader. Ask children to reflect on what they have learned.

Teaching points

Display the vocabulary of recipes and encourage children to refer to it to support their own writing.

Ask children to work in groups when evaluating the different examples of instructions. Get them to rank each text in order of ease of use and ask them to justify their choices.

📖 Homework ideas

Distribute Frame 3 Evaluating a Recipe among the class. Ask the children to use it to record the evaluation of their own example of a recipe that they make at home with a parent.

Name .... **Date** ....

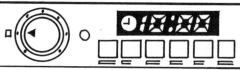

Use these prompts to produce a writing frame for your example of a recipe layout.

Title	**Heading**	**Opening statement**
List of ingredients	**List of utensils**	**Series of sequenced steps**
Diagrams	**Evaluation (how it turned out)**	**Illustration of final product**

Where these features exist in your example, label them in the correct order below. Add here any other features on your example that are not listed.

_____

_____

_____

_____

_____

_____

_____

Name ....   **Date** ....

WRITING A RECIPE 2

Recipe for _____

List of ingredients   **List of utensils**

_____   _____

_____   _____

_____   _____

_____   _____

_____   _____

Steps

_____

_____

_____

_____

_____

_____

Evaluation of outcome _____

_____

_____

Name ....   **Date** ....

EVALUATING A RECIPE

Explain the layout/organisation of your recipe.

_____

_____

_____

Are the instructions written clearly? Explain, using two examples.

_____

_____

_____

Does your recipe meet its purpose? Explain why.

_____

_____

_____

Does your recipe meet the needs of the reader? Explain why.

_____

_____

_____

Points of view

Persuasion & discussion

NLS   Y4 T3 non-fiction 17, 21

QCA   Geography Unit 8
Improving the environment

Geography Unit 21 How can we improve the area we can see from our window? Encourage responsibility in children – this leads naturally to a point of a view.

Lesson notes

During shared reading look at the local newspaper – an excellent source of examples of argument. Remind the children that they have already done work on newspapers in Term 1. Now look at reports on local issues and the letters page of your local newspaper. Make a list of issues of concern to the children and find a letter that reflects this concern. Read the letter with the children and discuss how the case is presented. Ideally your choice of letter introduces the concern, raises several points to support it, links these with reasons and concludes with some sort of statement of demand regarding what should be done.

During shared writing copy Writing Frame 1 Investigating Argument onto your board and write brief notes on another issue of direct concern to the children. Choose a topic like litter in the school, vandalism to newly planted trees or traffic problems at home time.

During group work give each group a local issue to cover. Ask them to complete their own copy of Frame 1 and whichever or Frames 2 and 3 is most suited to their ability, as discussed below.

- Frame 1 Investigating Argument. This is the frame you have just used with the class so they know what to do. Ask them to make their own notes on the frame.

- Frame 2 Putting a Point of View 1. This is a straightforward frame in the form of a letter that allows your less able children to concentrate on their sentence construction while still presenting a well-sequenced series of points.

- Frame 3 Putting a Point of View 2. This is a more complex frame in the form of a presentation to be read out. This allows the majority of the children to develop the skills required to reinforce their point of view. Your more able children can extend these skills by clearly linking their points.

Producing a final draft. Allow children to produce a neat copy of their work and send it to the appropriate person or organisation.

Teaching points

Use role-play to enthuse the children about their issues. Give different children the role of different characters involved in the issue. For instance, if the issue is dangerous parking, one child plays a busy commuter, one a parent with a pushchair and one a traffic warden. Ask each child to present their point of view in a different way.

Refer back to work on letter writing in Year 3, on page 73, and remind the children that a letter can be written for a variety of purposes including recount, explanation or complaint.

Invite local people into school who have an interest in the issue. Interview them and establish their point of view. Ask them to justify their point of view and provide supporting evidence.

Follow up work

The most important thing about work in persuasion and discussion is that it is real. Don't just do one lesson on an issue and then never revisit it. Instead, make it a regular feature of your class work with updates and reports, a noticeboard and replies to letters the children have sent.

Name .... **Date** ....

INVESTIGATING ARGUMENT

Introduce the concern

It is my belief that _____

_____

_____

_____

Points

-
-
-
-

Reasons given

-
-
-
-

Demand

I really feel that _____

_____

_____

_____

Name .... **Date** ....

PUTTING A POINT OF VIEW 1

B. Taylor
21 High Street
Rowndtown
TW11 5SU

Address

Date _____

Dear _____ ,

I'm writing to complain about _____

_____

I believe that _____

_____

_____

I believe this because _____

_____

_____

Would you please _____

_____

Yours sincerely,

_____

Name .... **Date** ....

PUTTING A POINT OF VIEW 2

Title _____

Introductory comments

It is my belief that _____

_____

_____

_____

Reasons

The following evidence shows that my belief is true.

- _____
- _____
- _____
- _____
- _____

Demand

I would like you to _____

_____

_____

because I believe that _____

_____

_____

Presenting a case

Persuasion & discussion

NLS Y5 T3 non-fiction 14, 19

Internet links
It is likely you will want to look beyond the curriculum for links.

Case for recycling – Friends of the Earth www.foe.co.uk

Case for healthy eating – British Heart Foundation www.bhf.org.uk

Case for nature – Royal Society for Nature Conservation www.rsnc.org

Lesson notes

Before using the lesson notes and writing frames prepare the ground on your issues. Some of this preparatory work takes place in PSHE, some in science and some in geography. The children should have already completed reports or explanations linked to the issue you choose. For example, if you look at recycling they may have already written an explanation of turning wood into paper.

During shared reading evaluate the way arguments are presented on the issue you are dealing with. Look at various formats including leaflets, posters, web pages and magazine articles. Discuss how well the case is presented. How is it introduced? What supporting evidence is given? How can its accuracy be verified?

During group or independent work give the children Writing Frame 1 How Effective? and ask them to evaluate a piece of persuasive literature you have given them. The first part of the frame allows the children to make spontaneous responses and mark the various features out of ten. The second part asks them to explain their first response in more detail. This forms the basis of further whole-class discussion.

Use the remaining writing frames to demonstrate to the children that there are two sides to every story.

- Frame 2 The Opposite View. This frame gives the children the structure in which to look at another point of view. If the presentation of the case is to be successful they need to really understand the opposite point of view. They won't agree with it, but understanding the principles it is based on will make their case stronger.

- Frame 3 Presenting My Case. This frame is deliberately placed last, as it cannot be completed until the children have gathered all the evidence they need to make their point and consider the opposite view. It is the framework for the final presentation of the case.

After completing the writing frames ask a representative from each group to make their presentation.

During the plenary evaluate the effectiveness of the presentations with the whole class.

Teaching points

Develop speaking and listening skills by giving plenty of opportunity for whole class and group discussion of the issues involved. Speaking and listening is not explicitly covered by the Framework for teaching and so we need to ensure that children still have many opportunities to practise their skills.

Homework

Send the children on an 'issue hunt'. Ask them to collect leaflets and information – from libraries, doctor's surgeries, charity shops and street stalls – on as wide a variety of issues as possible. Give them Writing Frame 1 How Effective? and ask them to complete this at home. Ask them to return it with the leaflet they have selected which, with the evaluation, can form the basis of a future plenary session.

Name .... **Date** ....

HOW EFFECTIVE?

The issue _____

Material

☐ Leaflet   Tick one box ☑

☐ Poster

☐ Web page

☐ Article

☐ Other _____

First impressions

How well is the case introduced?

_____

_____

_____

_____ ☐ out of 10

What supporting evidence is given?

_____

_____

_____

_____ ☐ out of 10

How do you know if it's accurate?

_____

_____

_____

_____ ☐ out of 10

Reasons

Introduction _____

_____

_____

_____

_____

Evidence _____

_____

_____

_____

_____

Accuracy _____

_____

_____

_____

_____

Name .... **Date** ....

THE OPPOSITE VIEW

The issue _____

My view _____

The opposite view _____

The five most important points

My view	The opposite view
1 _____	1 _____
_____	_____
2 _____	2 _____
_____	_____
3 _____	3 _____
_____	_____
4 _____	4 _____
_____	_____
5 _____	5 _____
_____	_____

Name .... **Date** ....

PRESENTING MY CASE

The issue: _____

_____

1 Thesis – my point of view

2 Arguments – points supporting my point of view

-
-
-
-
-
-

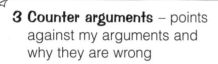

3 Counter arguments – points against my arguments and why they are wrong

-
-
-
-
-
-

4 Reiteration – a summary and concluding statement

WRITING FRAMES MADE EASY • Presenting a case • page 4 of 4

© pfp 2001 ISBN 1 874050 79 1 pfp, 61 Gray's Inn Road, London WC1X 8TH May be photocopied for use within the purchasing institution only.   **pfp**

Controversial issues

Persuasion & discussion

NLS Y6 T2 non-fiction 16, 19

Internet links
Look beyond curriculum links to where you will find more controversial points of view. For example,

Anti-whaling – Whale and Dolphin Conservation Society www.wdcs.org

Pro-whaling – Japan Whaling Association www.jp-whaling-assn.com

Lesson notes

The best way to approach controversial issues with children is through role-playing debate. These lesson notes help children prepare for a class debate on a controversial issue of your choice. Before the lesson ask the children to familiarise themselves with – and evaluate – available literature on the chosen issue.

During shared reading look specifically at leaflets on the issue. These are very useful campaigning tools and present complex information in a straightforward way. Make a list of the text features of a leaflet such as the style of language and the type of illustrations.

During shared writing plan out a leaflet on the board. This shows how important layout is to a clear message. Use an A4 format that is folded into thirds as landscape. This is a common format for leaflets.

During group work give each group a role. If the issue is whaling then one group could have the role of a conservationist, one a whaler, one a whale meat consumer and one could be a concerned member of the public. Each group needs to understand both points of view, produce a leaflet to support their view and produce a presentation to make at the debate.

Use the writing frames during group or independent work as follows.

- Frame 1 Seeing Both Sides. This frame allows the children to read material on both sides of the view and evaluate its effectiveness. Do this before they become too entrenched in their allocated role.

- Frame 2 Planning a Campaign Leaflet. Once the children are clear about their view, ask them to produce a leaflet setting out their case. This frame is for one side of the leaflet and is given as a starting point – give them more freedom over the layout of the other side.

- Frame 3 Presentation to the Debate. This frame provides the layout for the notes. It provides support for the speakers as they make their case at the forum. They should read out the final section word for word.

The forum or debate should last 20 to 30 minutes. Have three speakers for each side of the debate and make yourself the chair – the rest of the class forms the audience. Put the audience in a horseshoe of seats with the panel of speakers facing them at the front. You should sit in the middle of the panel. Let the speakers make their opening remarks and then let the debate begin.

Teaching points

Develop a collection of campaign materials such as leaflets, posters, badges, stickers and information booklets about a particular issue. This allows children to explore the issue in depth. Try to make the issue relevant to children's lives. For instance, drug education is undoubtedly of concern to children as they approach their teens.

Involving parents

Parents may need some reassurance that you are not brainwashing their children. Write to them beforehand and explain how and why their child will be learning to debate controversial issues. At the end of this project, which will take several weeks, invite parents to the school for a presentation by children of the issue and the work they have done to explain and explore it.

Name .... **Date** ....

SEEING BOTH SIDES

The issue _____

_____

One view _____	The other view _____
Who supports this view?	Who supports this view?
_____	_____
_____	_____
_____	_____
Why? _____	Why? _____
_____	_____
_____	_____
_____	_____
What material do they produce?	What material do they produce?
_____	_____
_____	_____
How effective is the material?	How effective are they?
_____	_____
_____	_____
_____	_____

WRITING FRAMES MADE EASY • Controversial issues • page 2 of 4

© pfp 2001 ISBN 1 874050 79 1 pfp, 61 Gray's Inn Road, London WC1X 8TH May be photocopied for use within the purchasing institution only.

Name .... **Date** ....

PLANNING A CAMPAIGN LEAFLET

Illustration

What we want

Title:

Illustration

Some facts

Our view

Diagram

Name .... **Date** ....

PRESENTATION TO THE DEBATE

Opening statement

I am _____

_____

I believe _____

_____

I believe this because _____

_____

_____

The issue _____

_____

My role _____

_____

My view _____

_____

Evidence supporting my view _____

_____

_____

Why the other view is wrong _____

_____

_____

Onomatopoeia

Poetry

NLS   Y3 T3 fiction & poetry 7, 15

QCA   Avoid tenuous curriculum links with poetry. There are, however, many onomatopoeic words related to weather. You can link this to Geography Unit 7 Weather around the world or Geography Unit 16 What's in the news? These develop understanding of weather around the world.

Lesson notes

During shared reading provide opportunities to hear and read onomatopoeic poems. Model reading these poems effectively by using expression, volume and intonation. Encourage discussion and response. Ask children to express – and justify – their preferences. Encourage them to enjoy playing with the sounds of language.

Highlight examples of onomatopoeia and ask children what they notice. Develop their answers, if necessary, to ensure that they understand that onomatopoeic words imitate the sound they describe and create mood and meaning. Use these examples to begin a class chart of onomatopoeic words. Encourage children to add further words to the list from other examples of poems.

Emphasise that poets make deliberate choices about which words to use in order to create impact, effect and imagery. Point out where onomatopoeic words have been graphically written to exaggerate their effect, for example hiss, written with a graphic emphasis on the 'ss'.

Children enjoy learning these poems by heart as by their very nature the poems are noisy! Support children in learning the poems by encouraging choral reading and by selecting poems with simple repetitive structures.

During shared writing model how to write poems using onomatopoeia to create effect. Begin by selecting an appropriately noisy topic, for example a storm or a fireworks display. Use first-hand experience of these events together with pictorial or video images to generate a list of onomatopoeic words. Also use your list of vocabulary collected during the shared reading of these poems. Discuss how to use layout and graphics to emphasise the impact of these words.

During group work use the three frames to support the writing of an onomatopoeic poem.

- Frame 1 Noisy Words. Ask children to complete this frame with a partner. Provide visual images to stimulate the generation and selection of vocabulary for their poem. The pairs can work on a class topic or each pair could have a different topic. The children then use these words to produce their own onomatopoeic poem.

- Frame 2 Noisy Weather Poem. This frame supports children by providing the initial verse in cloze form. They go on to use the remaining words to create their own verses.

- Frame 3 The Fireworks Fizz. This frame supports children by providing the initial verse in cloze form. They go on to use the remaining words to create their own verses.

During the plenary after preparation time, ask children to give a choral reading of their poem. Tape record the reading to enjoy again. Ask the rest of the class to evaluate the use of onomatopoeia to create effect.

Teaching points

Ask children to produce final versions of their poems complete with graphic images, perhaps computer generated. Display the poems on appropriately cut out shapes and then collect them in a themed class book.

Make links to the music curriculum by adding musical percussion to the performances. Link to the art curriculum by illustrating the poems with boldly coloured paintings.

Use this unit of work as an assessment opportunity as it develops speaking and listening skills.

 Homework ideas

Ask children to select a favourite poem that plays with language. Ask them to prepare a reading or recital at home to share with the class.

Name ....   **Date** ....

NOISY WORDS

Work with a partner. Look carefully at the picture that you have been given. List what you can see.

_____

_____

_____

List what you could hear if you were there.

_____

_____

_____

Look at some poems that contain onomatopoeic words and write down any that you could use in your own poem.

_____

_____

_____

Look at your class list of onomatopoeic words and write any down that you could use in your own poem.

_____

_____

_____

WRITING FRAMES MADE EASY • Onomatopoeia • page 2 of 4   pfp

© pfp 2001 ISBN 1 874050 79 1 pfp, 61 Gray's Inn Road, London WC1X 8TH May be photocopied for use within the purchasing institution only.

Name ....   **Date** ....

NOISY WEATHER POEM

Work with a partner. Choose words from the bottom of the page to complete this verse of poetry. Read your verse to check that it makes sense and that the words create an effect for the reader.

_____ , _____ *go the raindrops*

falling quickly to the ground.

_____ , _____ *go our Wellingtons*

splashing water all around.

_____ , _____ *goes the thunder*

roaring loudly across the sky.

_____ , _____ *go the tree tops*

as the storm goes moving by.

pop	fizz	hush	strum	click	bubble	whistle
rip	slap	whiz	slide	splash	whoosh	crackle
hum	drip	whack	clap	splish	rustle	rattle
hiss	drop	crack	swish	squeak	splatter	gurgle
hush	bang	crash	creak	babble	slither	hum
whip	buzz	smash	slurp	splosh	flutter	sizzle

Now add your own verse over the page.

Name .... **Date** ....

THE FIREWORKS FIZZ

Work with a partner. Choose words from the bottom of the page to complete this verse of poetry. Read your verse to check that it makes sense and that the words create an effect for the reader.

The _____ of Catherine wheels that _____ and _____ ,

The _____ of sausages that _____ in the pan,

The flames of the bonfire that _____ and _____ ,

These are the things that bonfire nights are made of.

Now go on to create your own verse using the words below to help you.

_____

_____

_____

_____

_____

pop	drip	crack	creak	sizzle	whistle
hum	drop	crash	click	bubble	crackle
hiss	bang	smash	splash	whoosh	rattle
hush	buzz	clang	splish	rustle	hum
whip	hush	slide	squeak	splatter	gurgle
fizz	whiz	clap	babble	slither	slurp
slap	whack	swish	splosh	flutter	purr

Sequence of poems

Poetry

NLS Y6 T3 fiction & poetry 2, 3, 4, 13

QCA Literacy objectives suggest poems about seasons and months of the year – not relating to Y6 QCA schemes of work. Geography Unit 14 Investigating Rivers focuses on the water cycle. This could be the subject of a series of poems.

Lesson notes

During shared reading explore a range of poems linked by theme or form. Allow time for discussion. Ask children to

- identify the links, for example between form, purpose and audience. They may spot that ballads are traditionally historical poems while haikus are traditionally about nature.

- investigate how the themes have been developed, for example by spotting and collecting language related to the theme

- compare poems about the same subject but in different forms

- compare poems in the same form but about different subjects

- compare and evaluate the poems and the style of the poets in creating impact

- justify their personal preferences with reference to the texts.

Produce a list of text features for the different poetry forms or refer back to text features produced during previous terms' work. Keep the focus on poetry forms that the children have experienced before.

During shared writing and over several lessons, revise with the children how to plan, draft and edit poems in a variety of forms. Model the selection of subject matter, form and vocabulary.

Model the writing of the first verse of a poem in the series you have chosen, for example a ballad. Collaboratively produce the second verse, with the remaining verses to be completed by children working in groups during independent activities.

Link these poems by theme and/or form. Select a subject matter that lends itself to serialisation and relates to children's first-hand experience, for example the months of the year, the seasons, the water cycle, the life cycle of a plant, animal or person, character profiles of children in the class or the typical sequence of the day.

To support children in writing in a given poetry form, use the frameworks given here.

- Frame 1 Limerick.

- Frame 2 Calendar Couplets. Children can compare their poem with 'The Months' by Sara Coleridge.

- Frame 3 Four Seasons Haiku.

Alternatively, use frameworks generated during the shared sessions or revisited from previous terms' work.

Teaching points

Hold a class poetry reading when the children have written their poems and collect them into a class anthology, grouped by form or subject matter. Evaluate their effectiveness.

Provide support before writing by

- asking children to remember and talk about their first-hand experiences related to the chosen subject matter

- providing visual stimuli such as pictures, artefacts or video footage and a range of texts related to the subject matter.

Ask children to transform an existing poem into a different poetry form, this frees them from having to come up with the content.

Provide a range of poems about the chosen topic from which children can collect phrases and words to use in their own work.

Follow up work

To familiarise staff with the poetry requirements in the Framework, your class can perform these poems in a 'work sharing assembly'. Keep copies of the poems, together with annotations to highlight their features, in a poetry folder for both teachers and other children to use for reference.

Name .... **Date** ....

LIMERICK

Work together to draft a limerick about one of
your friends. Use the following framework to help you.

Title _____

Line 1 (to rhyme with lines 2 and 5, to include 7 or 8 syllables)

There was a young boy/girl called _____

Line 2 (to rhyme with lines 1 and 5, to include 7 or 8 syllables)

Who _____

Line 3 (to include 5 syllables)

He/she _____

Line 4 (to include 5 syllables)

_____

Line 5 (to rhyme with lines 1 and 2, to include 7 or 8 syllables)

_____

**Now write more limericks about friends in your
class to complete your series.**

Name .... **Date** ....

CALENDAR COUPLETS

Read the first two couplets. Work together to draft the remaining couplets, one for each month of the year.

From January to December

January brings us lots of cheer,
As we all look forward to a brand new year.

February heralds rain and showers,
Waters the earth and brings forth flowers.

March _____

_____

April _____

_____

May _____

_____

June _____

_____

Complete your poem over the page and then compare it with 'The Months' written by Sara Coleridge.

Name ....

Date ....

FOUR SEASONS HAIKU

Read the first haiku. Work together to draft the remaining haiku, one for each season. Use the frame to help you.

The four seasons

Spring

Dew falls on the hill
Lambs suck milk, fresh and creamy
Flowers bloom brightly

Summer

Line 1 (5 syllables)

_____

Line 2 (7 syllables)

_____

Line 3 (5 syllables)

_____

Write the remaining two haiku for autumn and winter over the page.

WRITING FRAMES MADE EASY • Sequence of poems • page 4 of 4

© pfp 2001 ISBN 1 874050 79 1 pfp, 61 Gray's Inn Road, London WC1X 8TH May be photocopied for use within the purchasing institution only.

Story sequels

Narrative

NLS   Y3 T2 fiction & poetry 1, 2, 3, 10

QCA   Information Technology Unit 3e Email. Children use email to send and receive messages, in collaboration with another school.
Use this opportunity for children to write their story sequels for a different audience.

Lesson notes

During shared reading compare a selection of well-known traditional stories. Identify their purpose and audience. Explore and collect examples of typical language and text features, for example themes, structure, story openings, series of three events and endings. Identify the use of dialogue, characterisation, narrator's voice, simple sentence structure and typical phrases. Produce a class checklist of common features to support children's writing.

During shared writing model how to write a sequel to one of these traditional stories using the same characters, settings, phrases and expressions. Brainstorm ideas and ask children, representing characters, to produce a freeze frame of the last scene of the story. They can then change position to show what happens next. Repeat this a few times to build up the storyline for the sequel. Record each key change pictorially onto a storyboard. (See Frame 1 Sequel Storyboard.) Ask the children to tell the sequel orally in pairs.

Next, model how to construct a narrative plan (Frame 2 Narrative Plan) before writing the sequel with the children. Support them in deciding whether the text should be written in first or third person, present or past tense etc.

During group work encourage children to use the storyboard frame, narrative plan frame or Frame 3 Sequel Story Map to develop the planning and writing of their sequel. Frame 3 Sequel Story Map requires children to pictorially plot key events in the order in which they occur in the sequel as a plan for their first draft.

After completing an appropriate planning sheet, ask the children to produce the first draft of their sequel on the computer. Send these as email attachments for the children at the paired school to print out, edit and return. Your children will take on the role of editor on receipt of your paired school's draft sequels. After receiving their edited version, ask the children to go on to produce their final version on the computer.

During the plenary ask selected children to read their sequels. Ask the rest of the class to listen carefully to spot features taken from traditional stories. Alternatively, focus on the editing process. Ask selected children to justify their changes by identifying the improvements that they have made.

Teaching points

A further lesson could involve the children in sharing their sequels with a younger class.

Use traditional stories as a model to enable children to experience success in their own independent writing. Traditional stories are short and contain a limited number of characters. They contain minimal use of description, simple sentence structure and easily identifiable story lines – and children are familiar with them.

Use the story sequels to make an anthology that can be stored in the class library. It will undoubtedly become a firm favourite!

Involving parents

Ask parents to help their children in collecting examples of traditional story beginnings, endings and phrases. Then invite parents in to share in a reading of the story sequels.

Name .... **Date** ....

SEQUEL STORYBOARD

In the boxes below, draw each event in your sequel in the correct order. Add a sentence to each to explain what is happening.

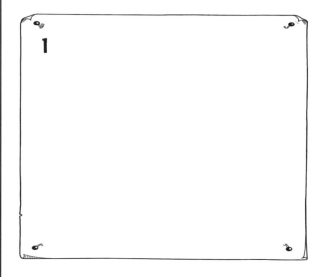

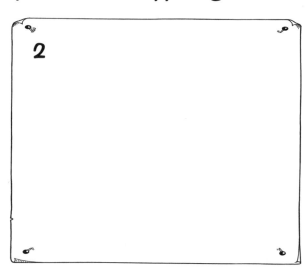

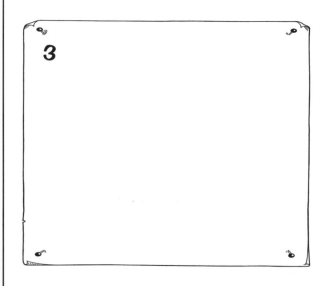

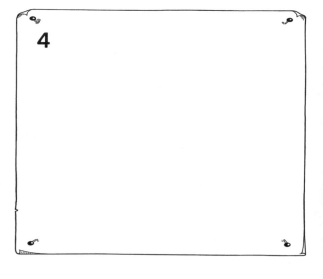

Name .... **Date** ....

NARRATIVE PLAN

Setting	Characters

Opening and typical phrases

First thing that happens and typical phrases

Second thing that happens and typical phrases

Ending/conclusion and typical phrases

Name .... **Date** ....

SEQUEL STORY MAP

1	2

3	4

5	6

Descriptive settings

Narrative

NLS Y4 T2 fiction & poetry 3, 10, 13

QCA History Unit 8 What were the differences between the lives of rich and poor people in Tudor times? This provides an opportunity for extended narrative and diary writing. Children can attend to setting (Y4 T2) and historical character (Y4 T1).

Lesson notes

During history lessons use a range of sources to identify the characteristics and features of Tudor life. Use these to generate a bank of words associated with Tudor life. This will support the children's independent writing.

During shared reading collect and compare examples of different settings during Tudor times. Highlight how settings establish the place and time in which the events unfold. Find evidence of how authors create settings through the use of adjectives, adjectival phrases, imagery, similes and metaphors. Identify words and phrases that give children 'a picture in their mind'.

During shared writing ask children to close their eyes and imagine the setting. Ask them to adopt the pose of characters in the picture. Touch the shoulder of each child and ask them to describe what they can see, hear, feel, taste and smell.

Ask a child to sit in the 'hotseat' and speak in role as a poor or rich Tudor, describing where they live or work, for example. Use this stimulus to brainstorm words and phrases. Model writing descriptive sentences and passages considering your word choice and order. Model rereading to check for sense and effect. Provide pairs with a small whiteboard and ask them to jot down appropriate adjectives and experiment with an effective opening sentence for the setting. Share and evaluate with the class.

During guided/group work use the writing frames to support independent writing of a Tudor setting.

- Frame 1 Describing a Scene. This supports children in generating ideas for their independent writing. Children describe what they see, hear, feel, taste and smell when looking at a picture for stimulus. For contrast, give different children different pictures to illustrate home life, town life, country life or work and leisure for the rich and poor.

- Frame 2 Setting the Scene. This frame asks children to rewrite a bland setting by adding words and phrases. Use the class Tudor word bank to enrich their writing.

- Frame 3 Setting Starters. This provides a range of opening sentences for contrasting Tudor scenes. Ask the children to add sentences to each setting to reinforce the use of adjectives, adverbs and similes or to write a paragraph starting with one of the sets of sentences.

In each case, go on to revise and edit writing before publishing a class anthology.

During the plenary share contrasting settings and evaluate how well they inform the reader and create a mental picture of the time and place. Identify good examples of using adjectives, similes and metaphors to create effect.

Teaching points

Provide time for children to browse carefully chosen texts to find good examples of settings.

During art encourage children to illustrate their own passages – and swap their passages and illustrate each other's – thereby testing the effectiveness of the written description. Read a descriptive passage to the class and ask them to draw the setting as it is being described.

 Homework ideas

Ask children to plan a setting for a story by imagining they have travelled back to Tudor times. Ask them to describe what they can see, hear, smell and feel and then to open their eyes and write these things doen in four lists. They can then draw a picture of this place, providing as much detail as possible. Ask them to their favourite four adjectives to describe the setting on the back of their picture.

Name .... **Date** ....

DESCRIBING A SCENE

Look carefully at your picture and imagine that you are there. Use the boxes below to jot down words to describe the setting. The class Tudor word bank will help you.

I can see

I can hear

I can feel

I can taste

I can smell

WRITING FRAMES MADE EASY • Descriptive settings • page 2 of 4

© pfp 2001 ISBN 1 874050 79 1 pfp, 61 Gray's Inn Road, London WC1X 8TH May be photocopied for use within the purchasing institution only.

Name .... **Date** ....

SETTING THE SCENE

Rewrite this passage and make it more interesting for the reader by adding adjectives, adverbs, similies or metaphors or extra sentences that help describe the setting. Use the class Tudor word bank to help you.

Anne walked down the street. On her left was a shop. She went to the door and opened it. Inside, pies and breads were on a shelf. Anne could smell the pastry. She approached the counter.

_____

_____

_____

_____

_____

_____

_____

_____

Name .... **Date** ....

SETTING STARTERS

The small bedroom was unlit, save for one flickering candle. In the far corner a wooden chest, darkly coloured and richly carved, stood open.

The street before her was crowded and noisy. The many tall buildings stood in rows like soldiers standing to attention.

From the open window, Francis could see the fall and rise of the distant hills. Glowing red in the evening sun, the brickwork of the village church stood out on the horizon.

That evening after dinner I sat a while in the long gallery, listening to the merry sounds of the flute and the recorder. As I listened my gaze settled on different items in the room – the boldly coloured tapestries, the woven rush mat upon the floor.

WRITING FRAMES MADE EASY • Descriptive settings • page 4 of 4

© pfp 2001 ISBN 1 874050 79 1 pfp, 61 Gray's Inn Road, London WC1X 8TH

Play scripts

Narrative

NLS Y6 T1 fiction & poetry 1, 9

QCA History Unit 11 What was it like for children living in Victorian Britain? Children learn about life in Victorian Britain through a range of sources. They communicate this through drama. Link this to the literacy requirements of comparing a text by a long-established author with the film or TV version.

Lesson notes

In history lessons use the work of Dickens as a source to learn about the life of children in Victorian times.

During shared reading take a look at the dramatic conventions of playscripts and familiarise the children with the appropriate terminology, for example script, character, set, sound effects, lighting, costumes, scene and stage directions. Talk about the typical layout of play scripts and how action and character changes are indicated.

Highlight the fact that play scripts develop characters through the use of dialogue and gesture, that action occurs within the setting and tension is built up through the delivery, pace and use of sound effects.

Compare play scripts with novels. Identify similarities such as narrative structure and differences such as reduced description. Highlight the fact that play scripts contain instructional language as do recipes.

Demonstrate how to read play scripts – use expression and gesture, volume and tone. Let children practice during shared and guided reading by allocating them roles to read.

Read an extract of a Dickens' novels that relates to children, for example Oliver Twist. (Use a children's adaptation if more appropriate.) Select an extract that can be written as a complete scene with action and lively dialogue. Watch the extract in a film or television version and compare the two. Identify similarities such as characters and story lines and differences such as the loss of the narrator. Make links between the extract and the film, for example setting, plot, number of scenes, characters, action and dialogue.

During shared writing sessions use an OHT copy of the extract. Model how to transform this into a play script. Using different coloured pens, underline dialogue and references to the setting. Identify scene changes and where sound effects and stage directions might be needed. Help children see that some parts can be deleted because of the visual impact of a play. Use these annotations to create a simple play script.

During group writing support children in preparing their own section of the story as a script. Provide a list of script features and have some examples of plays available at the children's reading levels. Different groups could work on different parts of the story.

- Frame 1 Play Script Plan. Use this to summarise the details of the original narrative and plan the play script.

- Frame 2 Play Script. Use this to transfer the details from the plan.

Allow time for each group to rehearse a reading of their scene.

During the plenary ask each group to read the book extract and then their script. Ask the rest of the class to evaluate the transformation from narrative to script and suggest improvements to the script or the reading.

Teaching points

Put on a performance to conclude the history topic – complete with costumes and props. Play scripts are a powerful text form, enabling children to draw on all their literacy skills – reading, writing, speaking and listening. A finale performance is a wonderful way to demonstrate all they have learnt.

 Homework Ideas

As suggested in the History Unit, encourage children to write a script for a conversation between two Victorian children, one from school and one from a factory. By including historical detail, children can demonstrate their understanding of Victorian life. Use Frame 3 Victorian Children – Charlie Meets Mary to support this.

Name ....   **Date** ....

PLAY SCRIPT PLAN

1 The title of the play

2 Details of the set/setting

3 Details of the cast/characters, their name and a brief description of each

4 The scene name and number

5 The main events needing stage directions

6 The characters involved in dialogue

7 Other – sound effects, lighting and costumes, etc.

Name .... **Date** ....

PLAY SCRIPT TEMPLATE

Title

Details of the set/setting

Details of the cast/characters (their name, a brief description of each and a description of their costume)

Scene name and number

Script (remember to include names of characters, dialogue, stage directions for the action, sound effects and lighting)

Name ....   **Date** ....

VICTORIAN CHILDREN – CHARLIE MEETS MARY

Details of the setting

Details of the cast/characters (add a brief description of each and a description
of their costumes)

Charlie –

Mary –

Script (remember to include names of characters, dialogue, stage directions for
the action, sound effects and lighting)